MORE POWER IN THE PULPIT

Other books by Cleophus J. LaRue
from Westminster John Knox Press

The Heart of Black Preaching

*Power in the Pulpit: How America's Most Effective Black Preachers
Prepare Their Sermons,* editor

*This Is My Story: Testimonies & Sermons of Black Women
in Ministry,* editor

MORE POWER IN THE PULPIT

How America's Most Effective Black Preachers Prepare Their Sermons

CLEOPHUS J. LaRue

Editor

WESTMINSTER
JOHN KNOX PRESS
LOUISVILLE · KENTUCKY

Unless otherwise indicated, Scripture quotations are from the New Revised Standard Version of the Bible, copyright © 1989 by the Division of Christian Education of the National Council of the Churches of Christ in the U.S.A., and are used by permission.

Scripture quotations marked NIV are from *The Holy Bible, New International Version.* Copyright © 1973, 1978, 1984 International Bible Society. Used by permission of Zondervan Bible Publishers.

Book design by Drew Stevens
Cover design by designpointinc.com

First edition
Published by Westminster John Knox Press
Louisville, Kentucky

This book is printed on acid-free paper that meets the American National Standards Institute Z39.48 standard. ∞

PRINTED IN THE UNITED STATES OF AMERICA

09 10 11 12 13 14 15 16 17 18—10 9 8 7 6 5 4 3 2 1

Library of Congress Cataloging-in-Publication Data

More power in the pulpit : how America's most effective Black preachers prepare their sermons /
    Cleophus J. LaRue, editor. — 1st ed.
        p. cm.
    ISBN 978-0-664-23278-8 (alk. paper)
    1. Sermons, American—African American authors.   2. African American preaching.   I. LaRue,
Cleophus James, 1953–
    BV4241.5.P67 2009
    251.0089′96073—dc22
                                                                          2008039366

Contents

Contributors

Willette Alyce Burgie-Bryant is a native of Queens, New York. She began preaching in 1978 while at Boston University. She holds a Bachelor of Science degree in elementary education and special education. Burgie-Bryant also earned her Master of Social Work degree from Boston University before going on to Colgate Rochester Divinity School in New York, where she earned her Master of Divinity degree. She holds a ThM degree from Princeton Theological Seminary. After occupying a faculty position in Christian Ethics at Wesley Theological Seiminary in Washington, DC, she was engaged in full-time ministry on the staff of Triumph Baptist Church in Philadelphia. She served as founding pastor for several years of Living Water Christian Tabernacle in Philadelphia. In 2003 she was named Director of Student Formation and Seminary Chaplain at Palmer Theological Seminary of Eastern University.

William S. Epps is pastor of Second Baptist Church of Los Angeles, California. A third-generation preacher, he is a native of Rochester, New York. His preparation for ministry began with a Bachelor of Science degree from Bishop College in Dallas, Texas, 1966; a Master of Divinity degree from Union Theological Seminary in New York, 1969; and a Master of Education degree from Columbia University, New York, 1970. He received the Doctor of Ministry degree at St. Mary's Seminary and University in Baltimore, Maryland, in 1987. He has also been the pastor of the Calvary Baptist Church of Haverhill, Massachusetts; First Baptist Church of Winston-Salem, North Carolina; and the Second Baptist Church of Detroit, Michigan. Active in the Baptist World Alliance and the Progressive National Baptist, Epps is the author of a daily devotional titled *What Did Jesus Say?*

Veronica R. Goines is pastor of St. Andrew Presbyterian Church, a historic multicultural church, in Marin City, California. In 1995, after a fourteen-year career in graphic design and illustration, she earned a Master of Divinity degree from San Francisco Theological Seminary. Months later she accepted a call to St. Andrew's. She has also served as intern supervisor for San Francisco Theological Seminary and co-dean in the Frist Call Newly Ordained Pastors Seminar in the Synod of the Pacific. She recently completed a three-year term on the council of the Presbytery of the Redwoods, serving as vice-moderator and moderator, consecutively. She currently serves as spiritual faculty in the Presbyterian CREDO program.

Cynthia L. Hale is the founding and senior pastor of the Ray of Hope Christian Church in Decatur, Georgia. Ray of Hope has an active membership of 5,000 with an average of 1,500 in worship each Sunday morning. She is a native of Roanoke, Virginia. She received her Bachelor of Arts degree from Hollins College in Virginia, and she holds a Master of Divinity degree from Duke University. Her Doctor of Ministry degree is from United Theological Seminary in Dayton, Ohio. Dr. Hale was privileged to be the first woman to serve as Chaplain of the Day for the opening session of the Georgia State Senate in January 2004. She serves on numerous boards and commissions. She was elected to the office of necrologists for the Hampton Ministers' Conference in June of 2006.

C. E. McLain is pastor of the Little Union Baptist Church in Shreveport, Louisiana. He was born in Ruston, Louisiana, and holds a Bachelor of Science degree from Southern University in Baton Rouge, Louisiana; a Master of Divinity degree from Brite Divinity School in Ft. Worth, Texas; and a Doctor of Divinity degree from Drew University in Madison, New Jersey. McLain has pastored churches in Louisiana, Texas, and Missouri. In 1991, McLain succeeded his father as pastor of the Little Union Baptist Church. He is the author of several books, including *Getting Your Own Steeple* and *Until the Men Sit Down*, and is coauthor of *A Legacy of Preaching*.

Otis Moss Jr. is pastor of the Mount Olivet Institutional Baptist Church in Cleveland, Ohio. He is former Chair of the Morehouse College Board of Trustees in Atlanta, Georgia, and former Copastor of Ebenezer Baptist Church in Atlanta. He is a national board member and trustee of the Martin Luther King Jr. Center for Nonviolent Social Change. He holds a Bachelor of Arts degree from Morehouse, a Master of Divinity degree from Morehouse School of Religion/Interdenominational Theological Center, and a Doctor of Ministry degree from United Theological Seminary in Dayton, Ohio. Dr. Moss delivered the Lyman Beecher Lectures at Yale Divinity School in 1995.

Otis Moss III serves as pastor of Trinity United Church of Christ under the leadership of Rev. Dr. Jeremiah A. Wright. Prior to joining the pastoral staff at Trinity, Moss served as pastor of the historic Tabernacle Baptist Church in Augusta, Georgia. He received his Bachelor of Arts in religion and philosophy from Morehouse College and his Master of Divinity degree from Yale Divinity School. He is currently pursuing his PhD at the Chicago Theological Seminary. He has done extensive research in the areas of African American culture, theology, and youth development. In 2006 he coauthored a book titled *The Gospel Remix: Reaching the Hip Hop Generation.*

Raquel A. St. Clair is the first woman to serve as the executive minister to the six thousand-member St. James African Methodist Episcopal Church in Newark, New Jersey, where William D. Watley is senior pastor. Dr. St. Clair holds a Bachelor of Arts degree in religious studies from Yale University and a Master of Divinity degree from Princeton Theological Seminary. She received her PhD in New Testament at Princeton Theological Seminary, where she was the first African American to receive the degree. Her academic and ministerial focus is biblical instruction as it relates to African Americans and specifically African American women. She is a highly sought-after preacher, speaker, and Bible study teacher for many church-related and community-oriented programs. She coauthored *The African Presence in the Bible: Gospel Sermons Rooted in History* and is the author of *Call and Consequences: A Womanist Reading of Mark's Gospel.*

Walter S. Thomas Sr. has served as pastor of the New Psalmist Baptist Church in Baltimore, Maryland, since 1975. He received his Bachelor of Science degree from the University of Maryland in economics. He earned his Master of Divinity degree from the Howard University School of Religion in Washington, DC and a Doctor of Ministry degree from Saint Mary's Seminary and University in Baltimore, Maryland. On January 31, 2005, twenty-eight ministerial sons and daughters met at the New Psalmist Baptist Church and voted unanimously to elect Bishop Thomas as president of the Kingdom Association of

Covenant Pastors as well as to the office of bishop. In July of 2005 Bishop Thomas was elevated to the office of bishop and presiding prelate of the Kingdom Association of Covenant Pastors. The Kingdom Association of Covenant Pastors is a newly established association consisting of men and women who have been influenced by the ministry of New Psalmist Baptist Church and Bishop Thomas. He is author of *Good Meat Makes Its Own Gravy* and *Spiritual Navigation for the 21st Century.* He is also editor of *Outstanding Black Sermons,* vol. 4.

Melvin V. Wade Sr. has served as the pastor of the Mount Moriah Baptist Church of Los Ángeles, California, since 1975. He was born and raised in Memphis, Tennessee, and received a bachelor's degree from Bishop College in Dallas, Texas, and his Master of Arts degree and Doctor of Ministry degree from Faith Evangelical Seminary in Tacoma, Washington. Before coming to Mount Moriah, he held pastorates in Dallas and Houston, Texas. Wade is the former president of the National Missionary Baptist Convention of America. An accomplished singer and songwriter, Wade is coauthor of three books: *God Is Good All the Time, God Chose to Save Us,* and *These Three.*

Introduction

While a majority of contemporary ministers learn to preach through preaching manuals and informed reflection on homiletic texts, many black preachers continue to learn to preach primarily through imitation of the masters. That is, they learn to preach by observation, participation, and an eventual mastery of the "how-tos" of preaching from accomplished artisans of the preaching craft whom they have come to admire and respect.

Learning to preach through imitation of the masters does not imply a mere copying of the style of others. It does, however, suggest learning by means of closely observing and subsequently mastering the dynamics that come together to make black preaching a powerful communicative tool in the hands of a master craftsperson. This preaching pedagogy is deeply embedded in the black religious psyche. In fact, it is so deeply woven into the fabric of black religious life that it becomes a part of the black sacred story—that story that lies so deeply within human consciousness that one is not always aware of just how forceful it is in shaping belief and behavior.

Consequently, the making of an effective black preacher begins not with formal studies but rather in the formative stages of the preacher's life. It is there that the black church molds and shapes a preacher's thought world in the richness and depth of the black religious experience. Owing to this reality, black preaching is not so much taught as it is caught. It is a way of being in the world that one develops over time by immersing oneself in the culture and norms of black religious life. One does not learn how to become a black preacher; one learns how to become a preacher in the black religious experience.

Blacks who learn to preach by emulating those who are representative of the best of the tradition focus intently on nine fundamental characteristics that come to fore time and time again in this style of proclamation. These fundamentals include (1) the hermeneutic of an all-powerful God, (2) wrestling with Scripture, (3) a sense of divine encounter, (4) a waiting congregation, (5) cultural awareness, (6) a well-prepared manuscript, (7) a fitting sermon close, (8) an openness to unplanned additions, and (9) a powerful living voice.

THE HERMENEUTIC OF AN ALL-POWERFUL GOD

Effective black preaching concerns itself with the extraordinary experiences of a people and their God. It also concerns itself with a people's unique way of understanding the Bible and of applying those insights in very practical ways. When one considers the historical conditions under which blacks embraced Christianity, it is easy to see how their sociocultural experiences would have a profound effect on their understanding of who God is and how God works out God's meaning and purpose in their lives. A central truth blacks quickly came to embrace when they were allowed to read and interpret Scripture for themselves is that Scripture revealed a God of infinite power who could be trusted to act on their behalf. This direct relationship between black struggle and divine rescue colors the theological perceptions and themes of black preaching in a very decisive manner.

A God who is unquestionably for them is what blacks see when they go to the Scriptures. Thus a distinctive characteristic of black preaching is what blacks believe Scripture reveals about the sovereign God's involvement in the everyday affairs and circumstances of their existence. African Americans believe the sovereign God acts in very concrete and practical ways in matters pertaining to their survival, deliverance, advancement, prosperity, and overall well-being. This is the lens through which they interpret the Scriptures in preparation for preaching. The preacher who would preach with a certain sense of authority and accomplishment in the traditional black church must always remember that at its heart the black sermon is about God—

God's purposive acts in and for the world. The most effective preaching is preaching that conveys with clarity and insight how God acts in concrete situations in the lives of those who hear the gospel. This is not to suggest that every sermon ought to have the word *God* in it, but each sermon should concern itself with God's essence and actions—God's divine initiative and revelatory activity, especially as that activity is manifested through the work and person of Jesus Christ, biblically witnessed and historically confessed. This all-encompassing hermeneutic is at the core of traditional black preaching.

THE IMPORTANCE OF WRESTLING WITH THE TEXT

Black preaching exhibits a high regard for Scripture and has historically been noted for its strong biblical content. In many black churches, biblical preaching, defined as preaching that allows a text from the Bible to serve as the leading force in shaping the content and purpose of the sermon, is the type of preaching considered to be most faithful to traditional understandings of the proclaimed Word. Indeed, it is no secret that the Bible occupies a central place in the religious life of black Americans. More than a mere source for texts in black preaching, the Bible is the single most important source of language, imagery, and story for the sermon. Though biblical literacy in black churches is greatly diminished from earlier years, it has yet to reach the state where the Bible's primacy as a rich resource for black preaching is no longer the case.

Thus, black preaching is inextricably tied to Scripture. In the eyes of the black church a preacher without Scripture is like a doctor without a black bag. In other words, what one needs to get the preaching job done comes with some kind of encounter with Scripture. Any preacher who seeks to be heard on a regular basis in a black church must learn some method of engaging the scriptural text and drawing from that encounter some sense of the Word of God revealed *to* and acting *on* the present-day human situation of the black listeners. Effective preachers recognize that this daunting task of creatively engaging the Scriptures and pairing them with black lived experience is at the center of their weekly preparation. Therefore the preacher must be familiar with the Bible. The in-depth knowledge of Scripture required of the preacher cannot simply be a task-oriented familiarity with Scripture, for the

Bible does not fully yield its treasures as the Word of God to those who visit it from time to time when fishing for a sermon. One has to live with the Scriptures and walk up and down the streets of the texts in order to have those texts speak forth with power and conviction. Black preachers learn early on to seek this kind of engagement with the text.

A SENSE OF DIVINE ENCOUNTER

Blacks believe they encounter God throughout the sermon preparation process and most especially during the initial stages of sermon preparation. This encounter manifests itself in various ways. For some it involves sitting silent before God while for others it is a "tarrying" for the Spirit. Something comes from without and buoys the spirit and sparks the creativity of the preacher as he or she embarks on the sermon creation process. Many attribute this creative spark to something beyond their own subconscious mind-set. They refuse to advance the preparation process until they have some sense that a power from beyond them is at work in and through them. Without this in-breaking activity many feel that the sermon will focus too much on process and not enough on purpose.

THE SIGNIFICANCE OF THE WAITING CONGREGATION

The people for whom the sermon is being prepared are never far from the thoughts of black preachers at the time of preparation. In fact, many blacks speak of their need to maintain a constant focus on those who will hear the message. In a strange way, the preachers seem to anticipate the anticipation of the waiting congregation. Thus, every effort is made to say *for* them and *to* them what they (the congregation) would say if they had the chance. Participatory proclamation not only influences the rhythm and cadence of their delivery; it also affects the interaction of Scripture and context. Effective preaching can only happen when pulpit and pew are united in conversation with one another. Owing to the prominence of participatory proclamation blacks learn early on the importance of the symbiotic relationship between the pulpit and the pew. Preaching is always done in community even when the community is not physically present at the time of preparation.

AN ASTUTE AWARENESS OF THE CULTURE

There was a time in black religious life when some people believed that the truly "spiritual" preachers shut themselves away from the world and descended from the mountaintop of their studies on Sunday morning to deliver a word from on high. Today's preachers warn against such aloofness and detachment from the world. They recognize the need to be in tune and in touch with the world around them. They sharpen their powers of observation by constantly seeking to name God's presence in every aspect of human existence. There is no distinction between the sacred and the secular in black religious life. The most effective preachers are mindful of the happenings in their social, political, educational, and economic surroundings. Many argue, in fact, that such an awareness actually strengthens one's preaching. The best of black preaching seriously engages the whole of God's created order in its beauty and splendor, its disorder and unruliness. There are no areas of human existence where black preaching fears to tread. To this end, black preaching can strike the uninitiated ear as harsh, intrusive, and at times offensive. Yet preaching that takes every aspect of life seriously has the greatest appeal among a large number of the black church-going public.

THE IMPORTANCE OF A MANUSCRIPT

While many black preachers do not carry a manuscript into the pulpit, most will tell you that to preach without a manuscript does not mean one is preaching unprepared. In times past it was believed that a manuscript preacher was an intellectual preacher, and conversely, that a preacher without a manuscript was a spiritual preacher. Such distinctions are quickly fading. While preaching without a manuscript gives the impression of immediacy, spontaneity, and anointing by the Holy Sprit, it is becoming more acceptable in black preaching to prepare a manuscript even if one does not intend to preach from it in the pulpit.

Writing the sermon out helps to bring focus and clarity to the sermon, prevents one from rambling, and firms up language written for the ear. A tightly worded manuscript, where each phrase has been carefully considered, helps the preacher to paint the mental picture more effectively. Moreover, a manuscript allows the preacher to get comfortable with the flow and contours of the sermon and thus serves to strengthen the rhythm and cadence of the oral delivery. To have the language of the sermon set down in writing and thus clearly set down in one's mind sharpens the oratorical thrust and limits unintended pauses and dead air in the preaching event.

Those who do choose to use a manuscript in the pulpit do so with great effect because the oral nature of the event is never far from their minds even when reading from a prepared text. In black preaching the style of delivery determines, in large part, the success of the oral performer. Blacks learn early on to steer clear of lackadaisical deliveries. Verbal essays that sound like a lecture in the pulpit are a no-no in many black churches. The oral delivery must be dynamic and invigorating. Spontaneity that allows for improvisation and digression even when using a manuscript is not only acceptable; in black preaching it's expected.

A FITTING CLOSE

One must learn the importance of closing the sermon in a proper manner. For some the sermon should always end in a joyful celebration while for others the most important thing is that the sermon end in a manner that is logically consistent with the controlling thought. On some occasions the close should cause one to reflect on faith and life. At other times it should move one to repent and to think more deeply on the mercies of God. The close might also call us to some specific action in the larger world in service to others, and sometimes it should simply issue forth in ceaseless praise to the wonders of a God who is for us. The closing of the sermon should not be a disjointed distraction or some tacked-on ornamental rhetorical flourish intended to whip the congregation into a fevered pitch. Rather, it should send the listeners away with a clear sense of what the preacher was attempting to convey throughout the entire message.

THE SERMON AS CONTINUOUS CREATION

In black preaching circles sermons are never fully completed. There is always more that could be said and will be said, since blacks have no qualms about preaching the same sermon again. The sermon is never a finished product. After the sermon has been prepared and readied for Sunday service, different ideas and new ways of thinking about it continue to come. Even while one is preaching the sermons, new thoughts and ideas come pouring out and thus become unexpected additions to the sermon. Many preachers edit their sermons soon after they have been preached in order to take advantage of fresh insights that come to them during its delivery or immediately thereafter. For some, the unplanned additions turn out to be some of the more creative parts of the sermon.

THE POWER OF THE LIVING VOICE

In black preaching the sermon from beginning to end is viewed as an oral/aural exercise. It is to be spoken and heard. The sermon manuscript is never regarded as an end in itself. What is written is but an "arrested performance" lying dormant on the page that can only be brought to life through the skillful articulation and mastery of the preacher's *viva vox* (living voice).

People who come from cultures with a high oral residue consider the spoken word to have great power. All oral utterance that comes from inside living organisms is "dynamic." Many black preachers rely on the power of the living voice to bring full expression to what they hope to accomplish in the preaching event. Blacks know intuitively that there has to be a certain energy and conviction to the spoken word when proclaiming the gospel. Ultimately, their ability to evoke, empower, challenge, and change comes not through that which they have written but through the spoken word—through articulated sound. An awareness of the oral nature of the finished product is a key component in the composition of the sermon. The performative component in black preaching is seldom frowned on by other blacks because of the importance they attach to articulated sound.

While one could argue that these nine basics and many more could best be taught in the formal classroom setting, in black preaching these observable phenomena continue to be passed from generation to generation through imitation of the masters.

This book reflects the continuing interest on the part of those who continue to learn to preach in this manner. It is offered as *More Power in the Pulpit* as a sequel to the highly successful first volume *Power in the Pulpit: How America's Most Effective Preachers Prepare Their Sermons.* The preachers in this volume come from diverse backgrounds, but they represent some of the finest preaching in contemporary black religion.

BIBLIOGRAPHY

Davis, Gerald L. *I Got the Word in Me and I Can Sing, You Know: A Study of the Performed African American Sermon.* Philadelphia: University of Pennsylvania Press, 1985.

LaRue, Cleophus J. *The Heart of Black Preaching.* Louisville, KY: Westminster John Knox Press, 1999.

———. *Power in the Pulpit: How America's Most Effective Black Preachers Prepare Their Sermons.* Louisville, KY: Westminster John Knox Press, 2002.

Oliver, Paul. *Songsters and Saints: Vocal Traditions on Race Records.* Cambridge, NY: Cambridge University Press, 1984.

Raboteau, Albert J. *Slave Religion: The "Invisible Institution" in the Antebellum South.* New York: Oxford University Press, 1978.

Rosenberg, Bruce A. *Can These Bones Live? The Art of the African American Folk Preacher.* Urbana: University of Illinois Press, 1988.

1

The Presence and Power of Christian Preaching

WILLETTE ALYCE BURGIE-BRYANT

I believe that Christian preaching is ideally a manifestation of God's own Presence, with power to have temporal impact from an eternal point of origin—that origin being the Word. If I had to craft a definition of Christian preaching, I would say that it is God's Word to a people in a particular moment, rooted and grounded in Scripture, directed by the Holy Spirit, transmitted through the personality of the preacher, proclaiming the love, grace, glory, power, work, care, purposes, and invitation of God in Jesus Christ.

Preaching is so potent and mysterious a phenomenon that my cumbersome definition hardly begins to capture what Christian preaching is and what it seeks to accomplish. The preached Word is something beyond the words of the preacher, since the preacher cannot control what listeners are hearing. As a preaching professor told me when I was in seminary, "You can control the *message*, the words that go forth, but you cannot control the *meaning* that develops in the minds of your listeners." Each listener's ear takes the message and translates it into that listener's life language, and God is in the midst of the listener's translation process. As a singularly compelling and dynamic preacher once advised me, "In the preaching moment, do not concentrate on the congregation; focus your attention on God. That is your job. If you do *your* job, God will see to it that the congregation gets what He knows they need."

All this has led me to conclude that preaching is a marvelously complex Word meeting between God and us, a meeting where things *happen* to God's glory, to the Kingdom's advance, and to our edification.

A dear brother in ministry once suggested helpful metaphors for the way creative sermon-preparation energy flows through two different types of temperaments: there are "Sergeants," and there are "Surfers." Sergeants are those to whom it seems natural (even if not easy) to abide by a regular, preplanned routine of prayer, study, and productivity. As the military title suggests, Sergeants are generally regimented in the way they live their lives. For example, Sergeants may be prone to having their devotional time at the same time each day; they may do a predetermined type or quantity of reading each week or month; and they may determine to execute the various preparatory tasks of their ministry on a predictable time table. Surfers, on the other hand, need the "tide" to come in for them to function at their fullest potential. Just like beachcombers do not legislate the tempo of the waves, Surfers' best work is fueled by a rhythmic rush of Spirit and creativity over which they have no control. When the tide rushes in, a Surfer is prolific and indefatigable, often accomplishing in days what a Sergeant might take weeks to hammer out. Oh, but when the tide is out, a Surfer is challenged, if not bereft: spiritual, intellectual, physical, and emotional energies hover at bare subsistence levels. During low tide, a Surfer is sustained only by the tidal pools and puddles of inspiration and learning left over from previous big waves.

Both of these temperaments require discipline and faith in order to function well. Sergeants must keep plodding on in the absence of the energizing power of periodic peaks of excitement, while Surfers must apply themselves to maintain basic functionality between tides. Even during seasons when the ministry vineyard or the soil of the heart seem to lie fallow, Sergeants must keep faith that the disciplined dailyness of their efforts will bear fruit in time. And Surfers, in the lackluster, frustrating, and even frightening times between waves, must trust that God will send the tides at the right times, over and over again, so that life and ministry will be fulfilled according to God's purposes.

On hearing the description of these two types, I instantly recognized myself as a Surfer. And I was enormously relieved because, up until that point, I had only heard of the Sergeant model and had been burdened all my life by the delusion that I was supposed to contort myself to function as a Sergeant. Now, I had the liberating sense that my task was not to be someone/someway else, but rather to be as faithful to God as possible in the context of how God had wired me as a Surfer.

As a Surfer, my devotional life has something of a seasonal quality to it. There are seasons when I am virtually obsessed with poring over Scripture, gleefully immersed in it, probing texts and reveling in the connections between texts and themes and concepts in the Bible. When I have reached a point of saturation, such a season may give way to a season of intense intercessory prayer, or it may transition into a season of ongoing, spontaneous worship throughout my days. Alternatively, I may find myself in a season of craving massive quantities of solitude so I can brood over the interior stock God has poured into me in recent seasons while I grope for insight and reach for deliverance. Another sort of season is one in which I find myself observing the world, reading voraciously, exploring a variety of areas of discourse. These and other seasons, each marked by the intensity of its own particular spiritual and intellectual appetite, come and go like tides in my life. The two constants, I must say, undergirding all these seasons, are the Bible (read or remembered), and prayer without ceasing. The transitions between seasons are a bit disconcerting, as I find myself in between one tide and the next, unable to focus on anything in particular and finding it difficult to be productive. At these times, indeed, I walk by faith in the One who loved me and gave Himself for me. It has been gratifying and calming to learn that God lets none of these seasons go to waste in my preaching life, each season in its own way making invaluable contributions to the sermons He subsequently sends to me and through me.

Perhaps because I am a Surfer, I have found that I do not approach sermon preparation the same way on a consistent basis. That is not to say that there are not some consistent practices that are important to my sermon development process; it is just that my *approach* is not predictable. Sermons are "conceived" in a variety of ways, and sermon "seeds" burst into my spirit and consciousness and lay claim to me from a variety of directions. The direction from which a sermon comes often determines, then, my starting point and approach. For example, sometimes while I am studying or meditating on Scripture, a fact, phrase, word, or image will arrest me. Occasionally a sermon will be conceived as I ruminate or pray over a particular problem—my own, someone else's, or a community's—and the Holy Spirit draws my attention to a biblical text that speaks, perhaps unexpectedly, to the dilemma of how to most faithfully face the difficulty at hand. Sometimes a biblical text will illuminate the spiritual or conceptual connections between events, relationships, or circumstances that until then had seemed unrelated. And then there are the times when some gracious soul invites me to preach for a particular occasion or on a particular theme, and I begin then to query the Spirit of God as to what He would want proclaimed in that place on that day to those people. These are just some of the ways the seed of a sermon emerges or is planted in my consciousness and begins to swirl around in my soul like a growing fireball.

After a sermon is conceived, there begins a completely delightful journey of sermonic exploration and organization, as I work with the Holy Spirit to have the sermon grow and take on some particular shape. I have found that several disciplines have consistently served in the development of my sermons: prayer, meditation, exegesis, research, imagination, and vulnerability. The way the sermon seed is planted in my spirit seems to dictate to some extent the order in which these disciplines are engaged in a particular sermon's development.

For example, if the sermon seed is planted by way of my being arrested by something in a biblical text, then I am first most inclined to "sit with" the text, prayerfully meditating on it to discern what insight, revelation, healing, comfort, or correction is clamoring to make itself known from inside the text. It is as if the text were very much alive, "living and active," breathing and compelling me to crack it open to find what it wants to show me. God is calling me, personally and directly, through the text, bidding me to lean my ear, my heart, and my life closer to hear what Divine utterance He would grant.

As a way of entering into the possibilities embedded in the biblical text, during this prayerful meditative phase I may use my "sanctified imagination" to construct a version of the feelings, motivations, needs, and impulses of the persons and groups in the text. This helps me begin to grasp some of the ways in which the text connects with universal human experience via particular circumstances. Cultivating some insight into human nature, through my own experiences and through the study of disciplines like psychology, sociology, history, and other social sciences, is very helpful in surmising a plausible picture of the unspoken, unwritten dynamics and impulses that permeate and surround every biblical scenario.

In preparing to preach, I try to exercise an intentional attitude of vulnerability to the text in my own life, allowing its encouragement or censure, its deliverance or discipline, to begin to work on me. To be sure, I am convinced that if we preach only what we have attained, then surely we are poor preachers, and that of a god no higher than we ourselves. Nevertheless, I consider submissive vulnerability before the biblical text to be essential for the humble proclamation of the Word of God. In listening to other preachers, I have found that such submission to the text injects an authentic personal energy into the proclamation of the Word, and further ensures the authenticity of the preacher in the preaching of it. Preachers need not speak specifically about themselves in sermons, but if sermons are preached *after* the preacher has submitted to being critiqued by the text, the preacher can proclaim with personal authority that the Word is true, lending an "Amen" to the authority and power that the Word has on its own. I have found, sometimes to my chagrin, that my Lord often wants to send a Word *to* me before He sends it *through* me. Of course, there are times when the Word really is sent through a preacher without necessarily being intended to speak specifically to the preacher; but I am persuaded that it is a good thing to keep the ego in check by attempting to hear what the Word is saying to *me* before I preach it to someone else.

Exegesis is the biblical inquirer's version of a treasure hunt. The meaning of one of Jesus' parables can be completely transformed by knowledge of some peculiarity of first-century Jewish culture, and the significance of some biblical character's words or actions might be hidden in plain sight until one understands more details of the historical context. Further interpretive vistas are opened when one does studies of key words in the Greek or Hebrew text—it is astonishing how much English translations obscure even while they communicate the Word of God to us.

In my view, an exegetical reading of the biblical text (which is a relatively modern phenomenon) must go hand in hand with a meditative reading of the text (which is how the Bible was read and understood for centuries before the Enlightenment). Not that both readings must say the same thing. Because it is sacred Scripture and because it is *text*, it goes without saying that there are any number of ways to read, hear, and interpret a particular pericope. But if the exegetical reading and the meditational reading turn out to be in conflict, it is then time for me to bear down in prayer, to find the deeper point of insight and understanding my Lord is trying to guide me to. I have once in a while been forced to abandon what I thought were some very comely and preachable phrases and rhymes when I discovered that a point I intended to make in a sermon was exegetically untenable.

There have been times when I have preached a sermon series. These sermon series were a boon to me as a Surfer, especially when the "tide" was out, because the series allowed me to sustain attention and momentum with the series itself serving as the "wave" I rode to the sermonic shore. Furthermore, there are few things more fascinating than what God will reveal when we return repeatedly to a text or a theme, asking again and again, "What else is there, Lord? What else will You show me?" The Bible is an endless depth, and preaching a series is a thrilling way to progressively plumb those depths in one specific area.

Where is the listening congregation in all of this? When invited by a pastor to preach to a congregation, I often ask about the nature of the occasion and its theme, the demographics of the congregation and the neighborhood, whether the pastor currently has any ongoing issues or concerns that are being addressed in the congregation, and other such background questions. Having access to these types of information enables me to be sensitive and informed as I try to discern what the Lord is communicating to me for the congregation's benefit.

After having been an itinerant preacher for many years, I found that preaching as a pastor is quite different from "guest preacher" preaching. For the four years that I pastored, I had a peculiar role in my listeners' lives as their undershepherd, and our relationship was a far more intimate one than can be cultivated on an Annual Day. As the Spirit led me to see the relevance of the Word to the intricate details of my people's lives, Scripture would come alive to me even more, and I did my best to pass that life on to my congregation during the preaching moment each week, as well as during Bible Study time. The context in which we worshiped together—in a house—also affected the shape of my sermons during that period. My house-church sermons often had a more conversational tone, as it was fitting in such a small space to have more of a dialogue together in the Word, along with the traditional "call and response." By preaching from both pulpits and armchairs, I have learned that there is a special energy and ambiance that can be obtained when saints gather in a space built and set apart for the worship of God, and another special kind of energy that emerges in a home setting, where Jesus Himself also did quite a bit of preaching. I have found that the worship setting does indeed affect the shape and rhythm of the sermons I preach, and I have seen God save and nourish souls through it all.

Birthing a sermon, like birthing a child, is sometimes painful. In the early stages of sermon preparation, I deeply enjoy the pleasure of savoring the biblical insights that simmer in my head while Gospel passion percolates in my soul. But it is often difficult for me to transition from these delights to the labor of choosing finite words and phrases to put on paper. As a manuscript preacher, I must repeatedly overcome the temptation to procrastinate at this point in the process. Delays at this phase are costly because every delay shortcuts the ripening of the sermon on paper that happens during the first, second, third, and subsequent revisions of the manuscript. This reality of sermonic ripening renders the preaching moment something of a still photo of a sermon that has, in effect, become a living organism, capable of growth and development, seemingly ad infinitum.

Though I usually birth sermons into manuscript, once in a rare while a sermon will alternatively come to me as an outline and then stubbornly refuse to flower into a manuscript, insisting on being preached from the outline. Still more rarely a sermon will drop almost full-blown into my spirit. Whatever a sermon's "final" form prior to the preaching moment, it is important to me that I take the time to become thoroughly familiar with it. Ideally, familiarity combined with a very large (16-point) typeface ensure that I will be far more engaged with God and the congregation than I am with the paper in front of me when it comes time to stand at the sacred desk.

Once a sermon is born and revised, there is nothing else here on earth to compare with the joy of proclaiming and manifesting the Presence of God to His people in the preaching moment. As terrifying as it is to stand in service of such an awesome God, it is also most life-affirming to experience God, in spite of my flawed and surfing self, condescending to use me in His work to save, comfort, correct, heal, encourage, and deliver His people. I am grateful for the privilege, and my life is sustained by the grace of it.

Sermon: "You Are on God's Mind"

WILLETTE ALYCE BURGIE-BRYANT

God sits high. But God is not sitting high and just watching the clouds go by. God sits high and is lifted up above every name that can be named for a reason. God sits high and lifted up above every principality and every power, above everything in all creation for a purpose. God sits high and lifted up above every demon and every destruction, above every disease and every distress; God sits high and lifted up above every imaginable sin and every affliction, for a meaningful purpose, and that purpose is so that God can rule and reign. God sits high because God is sovereign; God sits high and lifted up because *only* God is God, and beside God there is no other God. God sits up high, exalted in the heavens, swaddled in glory! God sits high—and God looks low.

God looks low because God is busy. God looks low . . . to make sure there's enough seed to be found when it's feeding time for the birds of the air. God looks low . . . to take notice every time a sparrow falls from the sky. God looks low . . . to design high-end fashions for the lilies of the fields, and for the roses in your front yard. God looks low . . . to count the hairs on your head, and my head. God looks low . . . to prepare answers to our prayers before we even recognize the need to pray. God looks low . . . to search us, and to know us; to see our lying down and our rising up; to get acquainted with all of our wonderful and nasty ways. God looks low . . . to see just which of the riches in glory in Christ Jesus each of us will need from moment to moment to moment, each and every day. God looks low . . . to wield the two-edged sword of God's Word, a sword so sharp it could split the bone from the marrow, so sharp it can dissect the intentions of the heart, a Word so sharp it can separate the need from the want, the real from the illusion, the foolishness from the faith. God wields a sword so sharp it can separate the sinner from the sin. Yes, God looks low . . . and sometimes, to catch a glimpse of us in all our low-down-ness, God has to look *really* low. But thanks be to God—God looks low, anyhow.

God sits high and looks low: God sits high enough to be in charge, and God looks low enough to make a difference. But why?

Why should God bother to extend Himself across the span of the distance between East and West? Why should God condescend to fill the void between North and South? Why should God reach out His arms of mercy and stretch them out till one hand touches heaven and the other touches hell. Why should God simultaneously sit high and look low?

God sits so high and looks so low because *you* . . . are on God's mind.

You are on God's mind. You *are* on God's mind. . . .

Listen to a story: The people of Israel had been overwhelmed by a foreign, hostile power. They were dragged away from the safe and the familiar; they were taken away from their homes and separated from their sense of independence. They weren't sure if their exile was more of a punishment for their disobedience to God or a test of their faithfulness and their willingness to trust God through adversity; it may have been a little bit of both. They found themselves in a condition that is not at all uncommon: they were under pressure—defeated, even—by an adversary. The Israelites were in a situation where there were no easy answers, they were in a place in life where God's intentions were not as plain and as clear as we might wish they were. We've all been there. They were in exile. You and I have been in exile too. Yes, we have.

When your heart is so broken that your chest feels like it's caved in and no one understands, that's a kind of exile: an exile from connection, an exile from comfort. We've been there.

When everything is going wrong and you have no power to make it right, that's exile. When somebody else is calling the shots and the shots are shooting you, that's exile. When you're cast out of your safety zone in life and have to find your way through hostile foreign fields, that's exile. Exile—we've been there. Exile is disconcerting, disturbing, and bewildering. We've been there, just like the Israelites. They were bewildered in their exile: not sure how to read the writing on the wall, not sure how to interpret what was going on, not sure what it was that God was up to. Exile.

Though He did not tell them His heart immediately, God did not remain silent in the face of the Israelites' bewilderment. Though He bided His time and chose His moment, and they had to wait for His Word, God did not tarry endlessly speechless while the Israelites languished in exile. No, in the midst of their predicament, through the prophet Jeremiah, at the right time, God told the exiled people of Israel, "I know the plans I have for you" (Jer. 29:11). The Hebrew word *hasab* is translated here as "to have a plan." *Hasab* is a word that is rich in meaning. This word tells us that God is *scheming* and *planning*, *plotting* and *contriving*, *counting* and *measuring*, skillfully and artfully *reckoning*, even now, for you. God's mind is busy devising *strategies*, for you. It means that God is *thinking*, and thinking hard, about you. God's mind has *purposes in its working*, for you.

"I know the plans I have for you," says the LORD to the exiles. "Plans to *prosper* you, and not to harm you" (Jer. 29:11 NIV). Now, in this context, the word "prosper" does *not* mean "make you financially rich." The word here translated as "prosper" is the Hebrew word *shalom*, and the word shalom is so abundant in meaning that it boggles the imagination.

Shalom here means that, if you would just get God on your mind, God has plans to give you *peace* and to make you *peaceful*. Shalom means that if you would just get God on your mind, God has plans to make you *dwell in safety*. Shalom means that if you would just get God on your mind, God has plans to situate you in *good health* of mind, of body, and of spirit. Shalom here means that if you would just get God on your mind, God has you on *His* mind, with plans to situate you in *whole and healthy relationships*. Shalom here means that if you would just get God on your mind, God has plans to heal and build up your *community*.

Shalom here means that if you would just get God on your mind, God has you on *His* mind, with plans to crown your Godly efforts with *divine approval*. Shalom here means that God has you on His mind to bring you out of exile, out of exile and into a state of fulfilled *well-being* in every dimension of your existence. You are on God's mind, and God has plans to *shalom* you, not to harm you, plans to give you hope and a future.

> Then you will call upon me and come and pray to me, and I will listen to you. You will seek me and find me when you seek me with all your heart. I . . . will bring you back from captivity. I will gather you from all the nations and places where I have banished you. (Jer. 29:12–14 NIV).

Yes, you *are* on God's mind.

Yes, you. You, brokenhearted one. You've been exiled to a dark night, a dark night of despair. A night so dark that your eyes feel blinded and the darkness itself feels thick. The darkness of your despair is so chill it makes you shiver, so heavy it makes you stagger; the dark of despair is so sharp it cuts your heart; it's so deep you feel like you're drowning. You're in exile in a land of despair, but I came by to tell you that *you* are on God's mind, and He has plans to bring you back from your exile. You *are* on God's mind.

And so are you. You, weary one, you, tired of trying. You've been dragged away, an exile, to a state of frustration. You tried and you tried, but your situation refuses to yield. You worked and labored, prayed and believed, trusted and hung on, but now you find yourself perched on the edge of a precipice that overhangs unbelief. God did not come when you wanted God to, and it's gone on so long that you're beginning to believe that maybe just this *one* time, God just might be running late. Well, let me tell you about a woman named Sarah and a man named Abraham; let me tell you what waiting on God and trusting in God's plans for you can do.

Sarah and Abraham wanted very much to have a child of their own, and they received a word from the Lord promising them that they would. But a long time passed—*years*—without any sign that God was going to follow through on His promise. Abraham and Sarah began to wonder if they were supposed to help God out somehow, or if they had misunderstood God's intentions. To make a really long story short, they did finally conceive a child between them, and it was a son, and they called him Isaac.

Needless to say, Isaac was the apple of his parents' eyes. Well, one day when Isaac was in his early teens, God told Abraham to take Isaac up to a mountain and sacrifice his son, his only son, his promised and long awaited and much-cherished son. God told Abraham to sacrifice his son to God.

Abraham wasted no time. He saddled up a donkey for the trip. He cut and brought wood for the burnt sacrifice. Abraham, Isaac, and two servants journeyed for three whole days until they could see God's chosen site of sacrifice off in the distance. At that point the man and his son left the donkey and the servants, and Abraham said, "We will go on ahead and worship." As they moved forward, Isaac noticed that something was amiss, something was wrong: "But daddy!! The flint for the fire is here, and the wood is here, but *where is the lamb for the burnt offering*??"

Abraham had to answer his son. And so Abraham, the faithful one, replied as all the faithful have learned to respond ever since. In times of want and times of scarcity, in times of short-handedness and short-moneyedness, in times of depletion and exhaustion, in times when visions fail and steps falter, Abraham's offspring in the faith have learned to answer just as Abraham answered. Abraham knew enough about God to be able to say, "God Himself will provide the lamb for the sacrifice."

God is willing to provide for you. God is glad to provide for you. God is wise enough to provide for you. And God is able to provide for you. But in order to be in the right place at the right time to receive your provision when it arrives, you have to get yourself situated in accordance with God's instructions. Watch Abraham:

After leaving the servants and the donkey, Abraham took Isaac and headed out to the place that *God had told him* to go to. And when he got to the place *God had told him* to go to, Abraham built an altar, *just as God had instructed*. Then, Abraham laid out the wood on the altar, *just like he was supposed to*. And then, in ultimate obedience to God, Abraham laid out his son, his precious son, his promised son, his long-awaited son, his only son, his beloved son. Abraham laid out his son on the altar of sacrifice, *just like God had told him to*. Abraham was positioned for blessing because he was faith filled and wise enough to follow God's instructions. And Abraham raised the knife to slay his precious, beloved, only son, to follow through on God's instructions and make good on his obedience. And just as he was about to plunge that knife into his son's pounding heart, Abraham was distracted by a noise. It was the sound of something rustling, rattling, struggling in the bushes. Because, you see, Abraham and Isaac were on God's mind, just as you are.

This is how God works. While Abraham and Isaac were making their way up one side of the mountain, God had another journey being made up the *other* side of the mountain. While Abraham and Isaac were making their faithful and torturous climb, a ram was making a journey to the mountaintop too. And this ram's journey up the mountain wasn't a trip God threw together at the last minute.

In order to be fit for sacrifice, in order to be ritually clean and acceptable, that ram had to be utterly unscarred and completely uninjured. To be fit for God's plan, that ram had to be preserved from the countless natural hazards in the life of a wild he-goat. God Himself had to stand vigil and keep that ram safe. God had to keep that ram safe from childhood injuries while it frolicked carelessly on the rugged mountainside. God had to keep that ram unscarred through the head-butting fights for male dominance that would punctuate the ram's adolescence. God had to keep that ram from even incidental injuries on the uneven and rocky Middle-Eastern mountain terrain. So God preserved that ram through a lifetime of dangers, toils, and snares to bring him, without spot or injury, to the top of the very mountain where, unbeknownst to the ram, he had an appointment with Abraham and Isaac!

But that's not all: God had to spend some time strategizing on this thing! Let's go even further back in time. *Centuries* before Abraham and Isaac were ever born, God sent storms of wind and sand and rain onto that mountain of sacrifice; sent storms fierce enough to wear down rocks; sent storms in just the right direction and just the right frequency to pummel the rocks in just the right place on that mountain so that in one particular growing season, there would be just enough soil in a rocky cleft to allow some seeds to take root and grow strong. So, after centuries of preparing the soil in that specific place, God caused some seeds to take root near the spot that God had chosen for the commanded sacrifice.

And these could not be just any old kind of seeds! They couldn't be thorn bush seeds, or the ram would get scratched. They couldn't be gentle flowering plant seeds, or the ram wouldn't get caught. God knew that He had to dispatch seeds for a kind of bush that would grow up big, and bushy and tangled, tangled enough and big enough to hang on to the horns of a spotless ram!! You hear me? God had to set some stuff in motion way ahead of time; God got some stuff laid out just right, so at the precise moment when Abraham was about to slay his only son, a spotless ram would find itself wrestling with a bush not too far off, calling attention to itself, making itself known and available as an alternative and acceptable sacrifice! You *are* on God's mind!!!

You there! Yes, *you*! You, Sinner! You are on God's mind! You may feel like you've been taken away captive into a life of sin. Sin has taken away your mind and made you an exile from righteousness, because the way you have been thinking and talking and treating people, righteousness has felt ashamed to count you among her children. You've been rolling around in selfishness, and your greed for comfort and pleasure has you desecrating yourself, debasing the sacredness of other people, and disregarding the sanctity of God's creation. You've been trying to keep God in a cage, and maybe you let God out for two hours on Sunday—or maybe you have been trying to banish God's Presence from your life and push *all* thoughts of God out of your mind. Sin has made you lose your right mind, and if sin had its druthers, it would also make you lose both this life and the next! But you know what?

Even though God may be the last thing on *your* mind, from the foundation of the world, your sorry soul was the *first* thing on God's mind, and you've been on God's mind ever since! So you need to follow God's instructions and get yourself situated into a faith relationship with Christ Jesus, because while we were yet sinners, climbing up a mountain of unbelief, Christ Jesus was climbing up the other side of a hill called Calvary. And when He reached the top of Calvary, He got tangled up and crucified on a cross to pay the cost to bring us back from an exile of eternal death! Jesus got caught up on the cross of redemption because God Himself had committed Himself to providing a lamb without spot or wrinkle to be sacrificed for our sin. On that Friday the Lamb of God died on that cross, and was buried in a borrowed tomb, but because you were on God's mind, and I was on God's mind, early Sunday morning that Lamb was raised *up* from the dead, with all power in His hand!

Be not dismayed, whate'er betide—you are on God's mind! Beneath God's wings of love abide—you are on God's mind! Through days of toil when heart doth fail—you are on God's mind! When dangers fierce your path assail—you are on God's mind! No matter what may be the test—you are on God's mind! Lay, weary one, upon God's breast—because God knows! God knows! God knows the plans that God has for *you*! Because *you* . . . are on God's mind. God *will* take care of you! Through *every* day! God will!! Over *all* the way! God will!! God *will* take care of you! God will take care of you. Because *you*. . . . are on God's mind.

2

Sunday Comes Early

WILLIAM S. EPPS

Let me begin by saying how grateful I am for the privilege I have been afforded to share the practice, procedure, and process that I use to prepare sermons each week to the congregation I serve as pastor, preacher, teacher, counselor, and shepherd. I trust that what is presented here will benefit those who perform and participate in fulfilling their calling to proclaim the timeless relevance of life in the power of the Spirit of Jesus Christ. As a preacher I live from Sunday to Sunday. My life is defined, determined, and directed by Sundays. I tell myself each week that "Sunday comes early." That makes me aware that my preparation process begins early as well. If you are not careful, Sunday will sneak up on you. Before you know it, the first day of the week arrives with rhythmic-like predictability, requiring what you are ill prepared to do even with your best effort. Before you know it, Sunday comes with the claims and demands of a waiting audience who anticipate something that you cannot guarantee. Before you know it, the time has come, and you must deliver what you cannot even credit to yourself if it works and that for which you are accountable if it doesn't. *Sunday comes early.*

There are more persons from whom I have benefited than I can mention here. I will list those who have had the greatest influence on me as a preacher. From my mother, Pauline Jacqueline Epps, I learned to be erudite and poetic. She had me learn poems as a child, which has to this day shaped the way I speak. Furthermore, I learned much from those whom I perceived to be effective communicators. From Adam

Clayton Powell Jr. I learned that it is acceptable to be uncommon and to have flair. From Sandy F. Ray I learned that presenting what you say with an appealing attractiveness arrests the attention of the audience. From Samuel D. Proctor I learned that weaving a story engages your listeners with images with which they can identify. From William Augustus Jones I learned that a large vocabulary is essential if you want to communicate effectively. From Gardner Calvin Taylor I learned to focus more specifically on one facet of a passage rather than bombarding people with more than they can reasonably appreciate. From A. Louis Patterson I learned to really appreciate the work of the Holy Spirit in preaching. I have benefited from all of them greatly, some up close and personal and others at a distance.

Moreover, there are those who are part of my circle of contact with whom I have been in close relationship, engaging in serious discussions and earnest reflection about preaching. James Donald Ballard and James C. Perkins come to mind. Furthermore, there are those I have mentored while teaching at Fuller Theological Seminary and while participating in a mentoring program at the University of Southern California. They have provided invaluable insights along with the insights of those who have come under my tutelage at the churches I have served. From Toussaint Hill, Calvin Banks, and George Lyons I have learned how to be relevant to their generation as I tried to educate them about mine.

However, the words of wisdom from my late father, Dr. Charles T. Epps Sr., have been the most important. I am a third-generation preacher. I have probably learned more from my father than I am able to articulate or even remember. Just being his child; traveling with him to conventions, churches, and meetings; hearing sermons from a variety of different preachers, and listening to him have all factored into who I have become as a person and a preacher. My father's advice, direction, and wisdom have been invaluable. The exposure my father provided has been irreplaceable.

I can remember his telling me, "Preach one sermon at a time. You have a lifetime to preach, and you can't tell it all in one sermon." Initially, I think I was afraid of saying too little. To compensate I would say too much. Dad often spoke of the necessity of prayer in regard to preaching. "You cannot preach without praying," he advised. He spoke also of the power of the Holy Spirit, who really preaches through the preacher to convict, convince, and convert those who hear about what God has done in Christ.

What I remember most is the importance of sharing the timeless relevance of the Bible. My father was always a stickler for the truth inherent in that sacred document. I learned to revere and respect Scripture for the sake of simply listening to what it says. Even as a child I would commit passages to memory whether I understood them or not, as I did poetry. I would come to know their significance later when as time passed I was made aware through some experience of their irrefutable relevance. The Bible is the book that focuses and guides the preacher, for we have no word/s of our own outside of the Word God has given to us in sacred writ. Preaching one sermon at a time, being prayerful, being Holy Spirit inspired, and letting the Bible speak through me are all basic to and in my sermon preparation process.

A memorable experience reinforces preaching one sermon at a time. Dr. Gardner C. Taylor took me out to eat after a revival service where I had preached. I must admit I was delighted and intimidated at the same time to see him in the audience. I trailed him through the New York City traffic, elated for this precious privilege to have a conversation all by myself with Dr. Taylor, an enviable opportunity to say the least. We arrived at the restaurant where he was taking me to get a bite. We parked, went in, and were led to our seats by the hostess. We sat down and proceeded to peruse the menu. After commenting on my ability to keep up with him in New York traffic, Dr. Taylor said without looking up from the menu, "Epps, that was a lot of sermon." I got the point immediately. I'd tried to do too much. I'd packed too much into the sermon. As the conversation continued through the meal, I was made aware that I only needed to let the particularity of a specific Scripture speak singularly with a clear and discernable voice that is unmistakable. To eat everything at a smorgasbord would give you indigestion, and one food may cancel the enjoyment of another. Everything on the plate should serve to accent everything else, adding to the joyful remembrance of the meal. I was left with this important memory from my shared meal with Dr. Taylor. With a sermon, being selective about the specific focus and having a central idea that guides your development will keep you from giving too much or too little.

Dr. A. Louis Patterson says often, "Holy Spirit you did it again." The real preacher is the Holy Spirit. Unless the Spirit preaches, no preaching happens. Our efforts, even at their best, are feeble. It is the Spirit that makes alive what would otherwise be mere words without meaningful effect or fruitfulness—however eloquently presented. This is the basic understanding that I bring to the preaching task, and understanding that comes from my exposure, experience, and education. I believe that preaching awakens and reawakens people to the reality of the reconciling, redeeming, restoring, and transforming presence of the Lord in their lives, in particular, and in the world, in general. Preaching interprets the activity of God in the history of the world and in the lives of people. Preaching reminds people of God's past activity as it interprets and reinterprets the meaning of that activity for the present time. Preaching interprets the will of God in times of crises. Preaching answers the question "'Is there any word from the LORD?'" (Jer. 37:17) and satisfies the quest for the One we most desire and need to encounter: "'Sir, we wish to see Jesus'" (John 12:21).

I have a clear, cogent, and concise description of the Bible that keeps me focused on heightening my awareness of the presence of the Lord. I developed my description of the Bible to guide me as I read it, study it, and contemplate its message for my life, for the community of faith, for the nation, and for the world. I rehearse it consciously and subconsciously so that it is there in my mind as I read the Word. For me, the Bible is the record of the testimony of witnesses who discover who God is, how God is, and where God is at work in the world. Those witnesses share their discovery of the presence of the Lord, their discernment of that presence in the particularity of the predicaments of their lives and the personal and communal development that resulted from their discovery and discernment.

A basic understanding of the Bible provides a thread of consistency and continuity that relates to my basic supposition about preaching, while guiding me through the process of preparation. This prevents me from straying into speculation that leads away from what is the essential message of the Bible in total and the specificity with which a passage or text is presented in particular. Karl Barth maintains that biblical faith is not religion. Religion is humanity's quest for God. In the Bible we are introduced to a God who condemns religion as idolatrous attempts to control and manipulate deity. However, biblical faith depicts God pursuing humanity. There is the call of Abraham, a covenant relationship established, maintained, nurtured, and sustained by God, who takes the initiative. The pursuit continues in the exodus event on through the wilderness sojourn, to the conquest of the land of Canaan and the establishment of the monarchy. It continues through the exile, return, and restoration of a remnant as well as silently through the intertestamental period. The pursuit of God picks up in a crib in Bethlehem, where the paradox of the incarnation stills a world in silence as an angelic chorus sings. It continues on through the life, teachings, preaching, healing, death, burial, resurrection, and ascension of Jesus. It continues through the power of the Holy Spirit to manifest itself even now.

We tend to believe that we invoke the Lord's presence by what we do and say. We are in search, pursuing as it were, the Presence we cannot see but in our heart and spirit we know to be. However, the biblical record depicts God pursuing us. This record of the testimony of witnesses pictures God coming in the cool of the evening for fellowship; God covenanting with humanity to bless the world; God making promises; God keeping and honoring pledges; God establishing, maintaining, and sustaining relationship with humanity regardless of the cost. The Bible has a timeless relevance that pulsates and resonates throughout all of its documents. There is no substitute for its enduring quality. The centrality and eternalness of the Word is undeniable. Our experiences do not interpret the Bible. Quite to the contrary, the Bible informs our interpretation of our experiences. Learning to permit the text to talk through me instead of my talking through the text is the goal for which I strive. Letting the Word find voice through me is my consummate desire. Because there is the tendency to interpret Scripture through the lens of our experience rather than our experience through the lens of Scripture, I have to be deliberately intentional to avoid reading into Scripture what I want to be there as opposed to what the Scripture actually says. I constantly remind myself to let the text do the talking. The timeless relevance of the message of the Bible transcends the medium through which it comes as it continually points to the source by which it comes, the Holy Spirit.

Furthermore, the people I have been privileged to pastor have provided ample opportunity for me to practice on and with them. I deliberately use the word *practice*. Lawyers are admitted to the bar to practice law; doctors are licensed to practice medicine; and preachers are ordained to practice preaching. Since preaching is not an exact science, preachers are nothing more or less than perpetual practitioners. All we do is practice over and over again. The more we try, the better sometimes we seem to get at it, but, let me hasten to add, not all of the times. There are those times when no matter how hard we try we seem to fail. We come to know beyond a shadow of doubt that "we have this treasure in clay jars, so that it may be made clear that this extraordinary power belongs to God and does not come from us" (2 Cor. 4:7). I learn more from the people to whom I preach on a regular basis than I probably realize. I know that they teach me how they hear. That is invaluable, particularly given the theory of communication that says it is the response of the listener that determines the effectiveness of the communication and not necessarily the intent of the presenter.

I am ever cognizant of my audience—their aspirations, desires, fears, hopes and needs. More so, I continually learn from them whenever the Spirit allows me to awaken and reawaken them to the reality of the reconciling, redeeming, restoring, transforming presence of the Lord in their lives. I also come to know that I am them and they are me, and we are all struggling to come to clarity about God, life, and our reality. I know that I benefit from preaching as much, if not more, than those who listen to the sermon. In every sermon, through the power of prayer and the Holy Spirit, I am continually awakened and reawakened to the reality of the presence of the Lord in my life, in the preparation, in the delivery, in the reflection on what has transpired, and in the attempts to preach sermons over again.

I begin each day by reading a couple of scriptural devotional journals. In this way I put myself in the proper frame of mind so that I may become aware of the ineffable Presence in whom "we live and move and have our being" (Acts 17:28 KJV). One of the journals that I use is the yearly journal that I prepare for the congregation where I serve as pastor. The purpose of the journal is to expose the readers to a passage, provide an explanation of its meaning, and encourage the readers to interact with how the passage is applicable to them. Positioning myself to experience the presence of the Lord daily through Scripture is for me a prerequisite for preparation. Permitting the Scriptures to speak to me without looking for anything permits me to be found by everything that the Scriptures afford. Just basking in the aura of what others have discovered awakens and excites me about *who* the Lord is, *how* the Lord is, and *where* the Lord is at work in my life and the world. Without curious speculation I simply accept what is related through the experiences of those whose testimonies I read.

After I read the journals, I read the lectionary passages. I became familiar with the lectionary in seminary, using it intermittently as it suited me, picking and choosing passages I wanted to preach without any consistency. Once as I considered the lectionary passages for a particular Sunday, I summarily dismissed all of them and wondered how those passages were suitable for this specific Sunday, the first Sunday of a new year. So I found something else to preach that I thought more appropriate. However, that passage kept haunting me and would not let me go, so I acquiesced and capitulated. On going through my routine for preparing a sermon, that lectionary passage spoke in ways I never imagined, convincing me of the merit of preaching from the lectionary. My appreciation of the lectionary has grown deeper because it gives me a broad range and a diverse diet of Scripture. Otherwise, I think I would tend to stick with the familiar, neglecting to discover the gems and pearls of wisdom that are contained in the whole of sacred writ. I am forced to consider what the relevant word is even from the difficult, seemingly inconsequential and neglected passages. I am made to be more inclusive of the Bible in its totality rather than just exclusive in its singularity.

I always begin with the Bible, as I want to saturate myself with Scripture as a seed that is planted in its soil so that I can be nourished by what it inevitably produces. This process enables me to be found rather than to find. It is like that old cliché that says, "A man chases a woman until she catches him." The reality is that I am not on a search looking, as much as I am being pursued by what will eventually find me. I put myself in the position to be found by what I am looking for by planting myself in the soil of Scripture. One of the lectionary passages seemingly finds me after a day or two, and I focus more intently and intentionally on what it is saying. I read it again and again and again in a variety of translations in order to get the different nuances each translation emphasizes. I ask myself, What is God saying through this word to the world? What is the relevance of this passage for this present age? What begs to be communicated from this word to and through the community of faith? What would be missed if we did not hear what this passage has to say? I operate within the scope of those questions unless I am otherwise directed by an insight that I receive while continuing my routine of musing and mediating on the meaning of the passage for the present.

I then consult commentaries to situate the Scripture in the soil in which it was written in order to determine why this word was necessary in the first place. Inevitably, a corollary emerges about its significance today. That gives me a clue about how to answer the queries that guide me through my process. Before I know it, *I am found by what I am looking for, a word that begs to have its relevance made known.* Then, I begin to narrow the focus by developing a central idea or a thesis statement that captures the essence of what is to be conveyed from this Scripture. A one-sentence description keeps me on target with the facet of the text I want to present rather than showing all of the potential facets that are there, thus blinding an audience with too much light. With the central idea leading the way, I

begin to outline what the passage has to say that is meaningful and significant for today. The outline that emerges evolves from what is in the text.
Each passage contains all that has to be conveyed. I become nothing more
than the medium by and through which light is shed that helps others to
see the importance of that word for them.

Then, I further expand the outline by focusing on how best to
develop each of the aspects or points contained therein. Continuing
with my daily devotional routine, perusing the Web for what is happening in the world, and reading, I begin to enlarge the outline beyond
its skeleton stage without developing a full manuscript. What began as
a seed is now beginning to grow a crop. I continue prayerfully to consider whether the Scripture is speaking through me or whether I am
speaking through the Scripture. Since I preach extemporaneously, a
full-blown outline helps me to capture the language that I want to use
to paint certain pictures, to emphasize the important nuances in the
passage that make its message unmistakably plain, and to harness the
significant correlation of the text to the present. I illustrate the message
with a contemporary instance and/or incident that in most cases is general in its applicability, or I use language that paints a picture that captures what is being expressed. Most often I shy away from personal
illustrations, as I tend to deflect attention away from myself in every
way possible. However, there are personal experiences that I sometimes
feel compelled by the Spirit to share as a way of being transparent with
my listeners, letting them know that I too am continually awakened
and reawakened to the reality of the presence of the Lord in my life.

When it comes to celebrating, which I define as "closing the message," I remember a quip that has been passed down from a time long
past—one whose relevance continues to last: "Good meat makes its
own gravy." The message inevitably creates its own celebration. The
goal and purpose of the message dictates how you conclude. Sometimes, I close with a song; sometimes, with a poem; sometimes, with an
illustration. At other times I remind the audience of what was said in
the message. Again, I remember the wit of preachers of another day,
who would say, "Tell them what you are going to say, say it, and tell
them what you said." What happens is determined first by the power of
the Holy Spirit and second by the uniqueness of the preacher operating
within his or her gift and skill set. I can operate only within the limits
of my ability and within the parameters of my capacity.

Before I know it, Sunday, has done what it always does: it comes
early. I ask the Lord to bless my feeble efforts, make up for my defi-

ciencies, and use me through the power of the Spirit to convey to the listening audience what God would want them to hear, know, and do. Then I go to deliver what I have received of the Lord through the Word of God, depending on the Spirit of God to use me. While I am grateful for how the Holy Spirit enhances what I attempt to do, I always sense that my first effort is less than desirable. I thank God for the privilege that is mine, to practice what I can never master yet what requires that I keep on trying. I refine that first effort by adding what I receive when I preach. Sometimes the sermon becomes part of the Bible study conversations and discussions. Insights from comments are also added to what has already been presented. I wait for another opportunity, knowing that I can always count on the "Holy Spirit to do it again." The process begins immediately for the coming week because, as has already been said, *Sunday comes early.*

Sermon: "Found by Much More than You Are Looking For" John 20:11–18

WILLIAM S. EPPS

INTRODUCTION

Easter changes the way we look at death and consider reality. No event is as heralded as the resurrection of Jesus from the dead. No incident has generated as much discussion about the consideration that life overcomes death. No occurrence has aroused as much reflection as to the possibility that life continues beyond what we know as the end of existence. Jesus did much with his life to expose us to what we would otherwise have missed. He offered us understanding, insight and light, without which we would be meandering in confusion, sadly disillusioned. He offered us salvation and the way to achieve what we could not acquire on our own. With his death, burial, resurrection, and ascension Jesus has, as Paul says in 2 Tim. 1:10, "abolished death and brought life and immortality to light through the gospel."

We gather somewhere between March 22 and April 25 to celebrate Easter. The date is determined by the first Sunday following the first full moon following the first day of spring. Given the issues that Easter addresses, it is fitting that the observance is associated and connected with spring. Easter comes at a time of the year when life buds and blooms, grows and looms, defying the notion that existence is doomed to a destiny of gloom. Now, that is the stuff of Easter. We gather year after year to celebrate a discovery that has altered our lives immeasurably. Even though we know the story well because we have heard it so many times before, there is still something about repeating it that captures our fancy with new insight and seizes our spirit with fresh understanding. This is one of those special days where "familiarity does not breed contempt," but rather deepens appreciation as it excites joyful celebration. There are those moments that always ignite the possibility of new insight, which brings added light to dispel doubt's night. The more we review what we have come to believe, the more priceless and precious the joy we receive. The more we reflect on what we have come to know, the more we discover we still have more room to grow. So each year we come as we have in the past, always delighted by the truth that lasts. Life continues to mount resistance to all that threatens its existence. Just when you think it has come to an end, it picks up and starts over again. Return to that time in the great long ago where you catch a glimpse of reality that defies fatality, pointing us in the direction of immortality. Relive the moment, permitting the experience of Mary Magdalene to focus your attention.

Mary Magdalene is one of the women from Galilee along with Joanna, the wife of Chuza, Herod's steward, and Susanna, who gave financial help and domestic service to Jesus and his disciples. She has been set free from what controlled her, and she was now in charge of making decisions for her life (Luke 8:1–3). Sharing her resources for Jesus' ministry and being available to go with him where he went says something about the abundance of her affection, the depth of her devotion, and the length of her love. She was present at the crucifixion along with Mary the mother of James and Salome (Mark 15:40). She observed the burial of Jesus (Luke 23:55–56). The fourth Gospel, which focuses our attention, gives Mary Magdalene pride of place as the first witness of the resurrection of Jesus.

Something dreadful took place that devastated Mary and the acquaintances of Jesus. One in whom they have put their trust and on whom they have depended was falsely accused and cruelly murdered. Two short verses described the incident with graphic poignancy.

> And when all the crowds who had gathered there for this spectacle saw what had taken place, they returned home beating their breasts. But all his acquaintances, including the women who had followed him from Galilee, stood at a distance, watching these things. (Luke 23:48–49)

The lives of those who were adversely affected were at a loss for what to do. All they could do is stand and watch. We are told that all the disciples fled except John, who was at the cross with Jesus' mother, and his mother's sister, Mary the wife of Clopas, and Mary Magdalene (John 19:25–26). The women who followed him watched what happened. What courage it takes to watch what you would rather not face. They did not run in fear. They did what they could; they watched. They did not hide in terror. They watched. Sometimes all you can do is show up and watch.

Following this horrific death, Joseph of Arimathea went to Pilate and begged for the body of Jesus and along with Nicodemus brought a mixture of myrrh and aloe and wound the body of Jesus in linen clothes with the spices as was their custom. Then they put Jesus in a new sepulchre in which no one has ever been laid.

> The women who had come with Jesus from Galilee followed, and they saw the tomb and how his body was laid. Then they returned, and prepared spices and ointments. (Luke 23:55–56)

The women began on what was left of Friday and continued on Saturday to prepare spices and ointments to put on the body of Jesus. Preparation suggests that the time will come for you to perform what you prepared to do. When the time came it was the first day of the week. What better way to signal the start of something new than at its beginning? It is fitting that on the first day of the week a one-of-a-kind, life-changing event occurs and a discovery is made. Events are dated by the measurement of time so that we can identify when something has happened. The first day of the week is an appropriate place to start again. That's what makes this day so special. It does not end something as the last day, but it begins something as the first day. Sunday is recognized as the first day of the week, and on the first day of the week there was a magnificent first.

The language used to depict the mood captures our attention with its clarity of expression. *Early*, *before*, and *while* capture the essence of the moment. It was early in the morning, before dawn, while it was still dark. It was early, before the sun appeared summoning the dawn, annihilating the darkness and dissolving the night. It was early before the purple mist that filled the atmosphere with its nocturnal hue would be dissipated by the light of day. There are times when we find ourselves compelled by some unction, moved by some stirring, pushed by some instinct, and prompted by some motive to do some things. We are drawn to do some things early, before, and while.

Well, as the story unfolds, Mary Magdalene comes to the tomb, and seeing the stone rolled away she runs to Simon Peter and Jesus' favorite disciple, presumably John, saying, "They have taken the Lord out of the tomb, and we don't know where they have laid him" (John 20:2). Without investigating she runs for help, presuming what she considered to be a reasonable conclusion. Those to whom she goes run to the tomb to verify her statement. Here she is seeking help and those to whom she goes are consumed with their own interest as it relates to her concern.

Isn't that the way life is? No matter what you share, the basic regard others have is how it relates to them. Driven by the intensity of adoring love and the enormity of abounding grief, Mary hurried to the place where the body of Jesus was laid. Anxiously driven by her allegiance, devotion, loyalty, and love, she made her way to the tomb. It is not clear whether the women thought that Nicodemus and Joseph did not do a thorough job on Friday. However, it is clear that they wanted to do their part. Mary made her way. She arrives and does not find what she was looking for. What she discovers prevents her from doing what she wants to do. That is just like life. We are disrupted by what we discover; we are prevented from doing what we intend; we cannot find what we are looking for.

She was looking for closure to an-all-too abrupt ending. She was looking to declare further her devotion to a departed friend. She was looking to add what she could to what had already been done. And she could not find what she was looking for to do what she had planned. There are times when we just cannot find what we are looking for.

Now, as Mary was looking, she was found by more than she was looking for. Wow! She did not find what she was looking for, but she was found by so much more. That is one of the major features of this story that clamors for our attention. We are found by much more than what we are looking for.

We are found by a heightened awareness that alleviates our anxiety.

Mary was lingering at the place where she had been prevented from performing what she had prepared to do. With tear-stained eyes due to grief deepened and magnified by a sense of failure to accomplish one last deed, she cries in disgust with herself and her situation. While she succumbs to her helplessness, she hears a question that is directed at her: "Woman, why do you weep?" She responds, intent on finding what she is looking for. "They have taken away my Lord and I do not know where they have laid him." Again, she hears the question "Woman, why do you weep?" She sees a figure that she cannot quite make out. She says, again intent on finding what she is looking for, "Sir, if you have taken him somewhere, tell me where you have laid him, and I will take him away." Then, she hears what heightens her awareness. She heard her named called by the One who could call it like no other. At that moment, she became aware that she was found by more than what she was looking for.

Easter's surprise is a heightened awareness that settles our confusion and conflict. We too can hear what we need to settle our doubt and calm our fear. Death is potent but not omnipotent. There are some things that death cannot do. Death cannot cancel the contribution that a person makes in a lifetime nor limit the length of the legacy that a loved one leaves behind. Death cannot erase the experiences we hold dear nor mar the memories that we keep near.

We are found by a helpful admonition that allays our agony.

Mary was told not to hold on to what she was looking for. You are looking for the wrong thing. "Do not hold me; I have not yet ascended to my Father." She was clinging to what she had to let go of. Do not hold on to this. It fades of necessity. Do not hold on to it. Let it go. You see, in a few days I have to leave this place. I am going to catch a cloud and ascend beyond time into eternity. I have to go, to vouchsafe what I have secured for you. I have got to go. My Father is waiting for me to return and assume my place on the right side as a victor. I have to go. Let me go. Hear the admonition that informs our understanding with what we need to let go of. When we exit this ephemeral reality and move to that bourne from whose shore no traveler returns, our bodies undergo a molecular decomposition and return from whence they came. Let it go. Let it go. Let it go. Life does not exist in a corpse. Let it go. "And the dust returns to the earth as it was, and the breath returns to God who gave it" (Eccl. 12:7). Let it go. Our hearts still cling to the body because it is difficult but not impossible to dissociate it from the loved one who dwelt in and animated it for us. Let what decays go. Death is not the end but the beginning. We can now experience the presence of the Lord differently through the power of the Spirit. We can experience the meaning of our loved ones lives like never before.

We are found by an affirmation that assuages our anguish.

"Go tell my disciples." Mary now has a hallowed aim that will direct her beyond what she was looking for. Now she has a testimony that will more than suffice for her life. "I have seen the Lord," she told the disciples. She now discovers that death, rather than discontinuing Jesus' life, has expanded his existence to be more encompassing of reality in all of its fullness. The affirmation that dissolves our anguish is that we have something to do. We have been commanded and commissioned to tell what God has done for us in Christ. Relate the meaning of your loved one to others. The best way to honor those we love is to live fully beyond life's worst as a testimony that their lives have invaluable worth. Our focus is redirected into meaningful activity. We have something purposeful to do. We have something to share that will make a difference about the life we view. God alleviates our agony with assurance that this is not all there is. There is something more. There is more to life than we can see and still more of life that is yet to be.

CONCLUSION

We are found by much more than we are looking for:

found by courage amid fear.

found by hope in spite of despair.

found by joy in the midst of sorrow.

found by light even in the darkest night.

found by love when hate has done its worst.

found by life even in death.

found by more than we're looking for.

Rejoice with these words:

Death where is your sting? Sting where is your grave? Grave where is your victory? He got up. God raise him up. He got up with all power in his hand.

3

Listening for God

VERONICA R. GOINES

I am the third of five daughters born to good Baptist parents, nurtured in the bosom of black church tradition. This tradition is what both underlies and informs my ongoing spiritual practice and my preaching. Prayer was consistently impressed upon us and punctuated every aspect of familial and congregational life. It was who we were as a family. Prayer was the portal to healing. It revived the congregation and infused the people with power to face the paradox of life. And it remains, all these years later, the underpinning of all aspects of my life. Prayer is the essential prerequisite for sermon preparation. It places me in the path of God and attunes my ear to the voice of God. Communion with God enables the excavation of the Scriptures and the discovery of the will of God for the people of God.

While sermon preparation is that spiritual practice of listening, waiting, and discerning, and one that I practice daily with persistence, it is a challenge at times to find and hold my center. Sometimes my thoughts race ahead of me; sometimes I space out or daydream, so when it comes to preparing sermons, I must bring my work to a singular and exacting focus.

I was always a student who needed silence in order to concentrate on her studies, and I find that I still am. My sophomore year at the University of Redlands underscored my need for quiet. I moved into a co-ed dormitory with my best friend and very quickly found myself confronted by myriad distractions. I found sanctuary in the school library. Thankfully, I am blessed now to have dedicated space in my home for the purpose of prayer and sermon writing. My study is on the fourth floor of my home, slightly secluded, with corner windows that overlook a tree-lined hill frequented by deer. Sometimes this view alone puts me in the proper frame of mind for sermon preparation. On entering my study, I experience a shift in mind and body, a signal that it is now time to center down—to turn my focus, attention, energies, and will toward God and God's Word.

In light of the many other responsibilities that I carry as a pastor, it is imperative that I schedule mornings at home for daily prayer and study. There is a blessing in giving God the first fruits of my morning energy. I do find that those things that I prioritize as being most essential to my life and ministry have preeminence in my day and are not merely squeezed into a hectic schedule. Mindfulness of my call and purpose supports the maintenance of this priority, although it is often challenged.

The Scriptures advise and shape my theological convictions about preaching. They bring me into remembrance of why and how I do what I do. Second Corinthians 4:7 reads, "But we have this treasure in clay jars, so that it may be made clear that this extraordinary power belongs to God and does not come from us." Paul's words speak to me again in chapter 12, verse 9: "'My grace is sufficient for you, for power is made perfect in weakness.'" Preaching is the most daunting responsibility that I face as a pastor. While being entrusted to proclaim the Word of God, I am also faced with my own humanness. I become, for moments, fixated on the cracks in my pottery. These verses help me to remember that God has made me perfect for God's purpose. God doesn't work around my frailties, but through them. It boggles my mind that God runs the risk that the world will know God through my imperfections. This is humbling. So my momentary struggles each week—and I do mean *each* week—subside in the light of God's Word. The same Word that intimidates me also affirms and continuously empowers me.

Another significant theological conviction inherent in Scripture is relinquishment, the spiritual practice of surrendering the results of the sermon to God. Isaiah 55:11 reads, So shall my word be that goes out from my mouth; it shall not return to me empty, but it shall accomplish that which I purpose, and succeed in the thing for which I sent it. My task is faithfully to prepare myself and to prepare the Word of God for the preaching moment. Only in relinquishment of all rights to the outcome am I effective in preaching. The results belong to God. Letting go of the outcome frees me to focus on my part and to trust God to do God's part. It is very liberating yet sometimes hard. I can't count the number of times that I stepped away from the pulpit thinking that, despite the hours of prayer and preparation, the sermon seemed to fall flat. Then I would open the doors of the church to extend the invitation to discipleship. For a brief moment I would close my eyes. And when I'd look up, there were members flanking me, stretched out before the altar, open, vulnerable, and teary eyed. And in these moments, God echoes, "It's not about you." The gospel of Jesus Christ is God's power unto salvation—period.

Jesus promises in Acts 1:8, "'You will receive power when the Holy Spirit has come upon you; and you will be my witnesses in Jerusalem, in all Judea and Samaria, and to the ends of the earth.'" God provides what is essential to the preacher, and preaching is impossible apart from the Holy Spirit. I once heard someone say that God does not call the gifted; God gifts the called. One need not be a charismatic personality to preach with power. One simply needs to be submitted to the Spirit of God. I am a pretty shy person, but in the pulpit I am absolutely aware of a power not my own that emboldens me to speak what thus says the Lord. Self-consciousness hinders my spirituality, but God-consciousness ties me directly to the source of power and strength and is sufficient to overcome timidity. All of these passages teach me that I am the mouthpiece and that God is the source of power and results. As I surrender to God, I become a participant in God's continued work of salvation and transformation. In the words of Dr. Cynthia Rigby, Presbyterian minister and professor of theology at Austin Theological Seminary, "We are the artists on whom the Transcendent has staked a claim. This is participatory, not transactional. God does it all, and I am fully included in the doing of God."[1]

It is deeply motivating to see evidence that God uses me to make a difference in the lives of God's people. I am keenly aware of the realities, the external and dramatic circumstances that press in on the lives of my congregation. Each Sunday members and friends come seeking the Mount of Transfiguration, where they may regain perspective and experience refreshment, and where once again Jesus may claim the center of their lives. What I know is that through the Word of God sung, prayed, and proclaimed, the same members who arrive burdened down leave lifted up. My purpose is to believe what I preach so that I can declare with conviction that "the Word of the Lord will stand forever" (Isa. 40:8b). Whatever the present and pressing realities are in the lives of members, they need to know that God has a word that will bring light to their darkened situations. They, too, are included in the doings of God.

Throughout my journey, from my childhood on, I have been actively engaged in the internal process of sermon writing. I was drawn to the Scriptures and easily committed them to memory as a child. I loved telling Bible stories and had the gift of embellishment. On reading or hearing a passage of Scripture, my imagination and memory would go to work to compose a story, weaving together biblical narratives and verses of Scriptures, integrating them into my own story, complete with illustrations. Preaching is the one thing I must do.

But it was not easy to transition to preaching out loud. When I first began preaching, I was advised to observe other preachers, to find one that I could pattern myself after. Although I did try this, it felt inauthentic to me. Then a mentor of mine, Bunnie Wilson, said to me, "Stay with your gifts." Her words were simple and profound. They spoke volumes to me. The person I really needed to observe first was me. I needed to get clear about my own gift-set—my personality, style, and uniqueness; and my relationship with the congregation to whom I preached. Little by little, I became more authentically who I am called to be. From the center of clarity about my own identity, I could benefit from the observation of others without running the risk of losing my unique voice.

Initially, however, I wrestled with being consistent in preaching. I was sometimes emboldened and at other times timid and sensitive to critique. My mother, the late Reverend Evia Goines, who was a powerful Baptist preacher, said to me, "You just need to claim your power." Just like that. Her words were a prophetic revelation. She saw in me what I had not yet seen in myself—God's anointing. I began to do just what she said—to claim and to live into the power of God in my preaching. It felt at first like I was faking it, "acting as if," but this taught me to summon my power. I now feel at liberty to go where the Spirit leads. My power is realized when I claim all aspects of myself: my imagination and memory, and intellect and emotion, my history and vision, and my strengths and failings. Power is three-dimensional. Nothing within the Spirit's leading is beyond the realm of preaching.

And preaching is most powerful when it is both therapeutic and redemptive. It must be existential in nature and theologically sound. The message needs to be one of hope, which ushers the congregation into celebrative worship. In *Shepherding the Sheep*, Benjamin S. Baker posits four principles that represent the essence of preaching in the black church tradition. Preaching must (1) convey the truth, (2) convert the soul, (3) comfort the disconsolate, and (4) challenge the complacent.[2] This model serves as a template for me in preaching, especially in a multicultural setting. Preaching is not an exercise in brilliant sermon writing but a means to convey the truth of God's Word in relevant and timely ways. In preaching, I am accountable to God as well as to the congregation before and to whom I preach.

While the origin of preaching emerges out of a dialogue between the preacher and God, the evidence of the Spirit working through the preacher is revealed in her or his sensitivity to and awareness of the felt needs of the congregation. My preaching is influenced, to a significant degree, by those listening. Through pastoral visitation, counseling appointments, the prayers of the people on Sunday mornings, fellowship hour, and the recessional line as members leave the worship service, I become aware of the needs and concerns of members, which I take to God in prayer. They are impressed upon my heart and mind throughout my time of preparation. They often become an integral part of the sermon. Whether through verbal articulation, demonstrative shouts of joy, uplifted arms, bowed-down heads, tear-filled eyes, or quiet contemplation, congregants participate in and assist the birthing of the sermon. The community is drawn in and carried along on the journey of the preaching event. One senior member, Brother Theo Barron Sr., who passed away several years ago, often prayed my sermons before I got a chance to preach them. He prayed them in his murmurings of thanks and his shouting out to God throughout worship. I would playfully accuse him of having read over my manuscript while I was out. The congregation would laugh. We delighted in the Spirit's confirmation.

One Sunday following the sermon, an utterly profound hush came over the congregation. We sat for long minutes amidst the palpable presence of the Holy Spirit when a voice pierced the silence: "Pastor." "Yes, Brother Theo," I replied. "Is it alright if I say something?" he asked. "Yes. Go ahead," I answered, gesturing for him to speak. And with joyous trembling in his voice he said, "I feel goooooood!" The congregation erupted into spontaneous praise. The origin of preaching may emerge out of a dialogue between the preacher and God, but its effectiveness is evidenced when the congregation takes hold of the sermon and carries its message beyond the preaching moment.

For the past twelve years, the lectionary has been my primary basis for Scripture selection. However, I always reserve the right to step away from the lectionary if led by the Spirit to do so. Most often, this happens when I am preaching a thematic series and the lectionary does not address a particular theme—although in many cases the lectionary has proven to be conducive to addressing thematic sermon series as well. More than anything, I have found the lectionary to be a good discipline for me. It keeps me from focusing on my favorite Scriptures and exposes me and the congregation to the breadth of God's Word.

Preaching in a multigenerational community that is racial/ethnically, culturally, educationally, and socioeconomically diverse requires me to use a variety of styles in sermon delivery. No one style is sufficient to reach a multicultural congregation. While I would say that my preferred style is expository preaching, I am also comfortable employing narrative, topical, and textual preaching. The Scriptures often lend themselves to one particular style of delivery or another, so I pay attention to what the passage is saying. For instance, is it instructive, exhortative, inviting, or commissioning and sending? If the passage enjoins the community in giving praise to God, it will most likely involve singing. If the passage addresses grief, it might contain more silence.

Never is the church more engaged and invested than when one of its members has a vital role in the proclamation of God's Word through personal witness. Several times a year I invite a member who has a lived experience of the point I wish to illustrate to give personal testimony as part of the sermon. The congregation powerfully resonates with these sermons. They savor and appropriate them in ways that cannot be articulated. In a home visitation with a woman named Mary Williams, who was eighty-five years old at the time, she shared with me her baptism in 1913 in the Mississippi River. I felt incredibly blessed by her story. I knew that I could tell the story myself in a sermon on baptism, but I was led to ask her to convey her testimony to the congregation. She agreed. The following Sunday morning I drove down the street, and there was Mrs. Williams standing on the curb waiting for me. She held her purse in one hand, with a cloth draped over her arm. In her other hand, she held what looked like a broom handle, resting it on the ground. I was tempted to ask her what the props were about, but even more, I wanted to be surprised along with the congregation.

Halfway through my sermon, Mrs. Williams shared her story. She had slipped into the cloth that had been draped over her arm, which represented the baptismal robe she wore at twelve years of age. The broom handle represented the poles that the deacons used to sound out the floor of the Mississippi River for the coming baptismal service. When they found a solid spot, they would form a baptismal pool by securing the poles in the ground and creating an encircled area. She waded out into the river and joined the pastor in the center of the pool. There she was submerged beneath the waters and lifted to new life. That day she made a vow to serve God all the days of her life, no matter what.

Her testimony continued through a litany of sorrows as the congregation empathized with her, mesmerized by her sheer strength and conviction. She lost her mother near the time of her baptism. Later in life, her father, who had come to be everything to her, also died. One of her sons was drowned in the Mississippi River, and another was killed in an accident. She reared her remaining children with the help of the Lord. At the end of all that, she reiterated, "When I was baptized, I promised the Lord that I would serve him all the days of my life, no matter what. And indeed I do serve him." Although she passed away in 1998, the vivid memories of her testimony continue to be spoken about.

I find that the community itself is one of the most effective resources for sermon illustrations. It becomes a vehicle for affirming, encouraging, and including members in the preaching moment. So I am always mindful, whether in casual conversation or formal visitation, to take note of the stories that I encounter.

Other resources and means of illustration are all around us. For me, it is a matter of paying attention and keeping my eyes open, with my heart attuned to God and to others. Nearly every book in my library is marked and tabbed with labels for easy access. I keep a visual memory of passages I will come back to and use in later sermons. I maintain a file of stories, poems, prayers, quotes, and liturgy, as well as articles on justice, spirituality, family, religion and theology, and anything I come upon that speaks deeply to me. I consult these files weekly and am constantly adding new and relevant material while eliminating dated sources. It is an invaluable practice well worth the investment of time. Even when I read for leisure, I come away with useful resources for future sermons.

For the seven years prior to my present call, I never preached from a manuscript. But I was led by the Spirit to begin to write my sermons down in the first year of my current congregation, more than twelve years ago. I then began to prepare manuscripts. But while I am scripted every Sunday in the pulpit, I am not anchored to the pulpit. The manuscript serves as a tool rather than a crutch. It represents only one half to three quarters of the preached sermon. The remainder of the sermon resides between the lines of the written word and is flushed out in extemporaneous delivery that draws on all my inner resources. The discipline of preparing manuscripts has been most helpful to me for a couple of reasons. First, it helps me to internalize the sermon. The process of writing, reading, and reworking the script helps me to appropriate the flow and details of the message. Second, the manuscript provides a record for future reference.

Recently I was compelled to read over a number of sermons from the past twelve years. It was a powerful experience, and I wondered why I hadn't done this sooner. In an instant I knew why God led me to write my sermons down all those years ago. Sermon manuscripts are, in essence, working documents. Even after the sermon has been preached, it is still being revised and rewritten, because God's Word is dynamic. I am beginning to go back and to rewrite sermons that I preached three to six years ago, with the benefit of new insight. These old sermons are life giving. I have found that as I mature in the Spirit and return to former sermons, they also deepen and develop with me.

Monday is the first day of my work week. It begins my round of preparation, inaugurated by prayer and a meditative reading of the Scriptures. Levi Miller describes prayer as involving the whole person in the search for God's will. I sit with God's Word not to exegete the text but to have it exegete me—to identify, name, and address what is present within me. I ask God to open my heart and mind, to anoint my imagination and memory, and to liberate me to see in the text what God sees. So I come, the whole person of myself in search for God's will, and I pray for the submission that can open and enable me to be a teachable student of God's Word. In prayerful meditation, I wait on God for words, phrases, images, remembrances, and even visceral responses. I pay particular attention to songs that surface, especially those that take up residence in my spirit throughout the week. They often augment the sermon. Sometimes they offer clues for the direction of worship.

When I have a Sunday free from preaching, I experience the luxury of preparing for future sermons four or five weeks away. Both the meditative reading and the distillation of the seed of the sermon allow for a more organic germination of the Word over a longer period of time. During this period my spirit serves as a filter, making me aware of and attentive to relevant sources that may be useful in flushing out the sermon, such as related passages of Scripture, stories, quotes, statistical data, or current news items, to name a few.

On Tuesdays, I also begin with the meditative reading of the biblical passage, deepening and clarifying the thematic direction in which I am led by the Spirit's nudging. At this point I will begin to cross-reference related biblical passages, paying attention to key words and phrases. Once I am clear about the Spirit's direction and have the seed of the sermon within me, I am free to consult other writers. This helps to focus my exploration and keeps me honest, so that I am relying on the guidance of the Holy Spirit and not simply regurgitating the words and work of other biblical scholars.

By Wednesday I am scouting commentaries, various periodicals to which I subscribe, and articles appropriate to the emerging sermon. My filtering mechanism is at work, helping me to remain more focused and attentive to material that will strengthen and support the direction of the sermon. Here, the structure of the sermon really begins to take shape, but its meat and muscle have yet to emerge. I am in a process of solidifying the core of the sermon, establishing its form—the introduction, body, transitions, and finally, its closing.

I liken the weekly act of preaching to that of childbirth—of daily needing to be intimate with God; of conceiving the seed of God's Word in the space of that intimacy; and allowing time for gestation of the seed, where the Word begins to divide and develop, like a fetus moving toward its predetermined identity. Following is the time of transition, where the birth canal is made wide and ready for the descent of this fully developed Word. This is Wednesday, a pivotal time in my sermon preparation, and while I am aware of the internal pressures to get it done, readiness for delivery isn't always apparent. I seek to nail down the opening for the sermon—that from which everything else will flow—and to come up with a word or phrase that will capture both its essence and the attention of my congregation. On this day I often find myself torn between allowing my prayers to devolve into seeking God for sermon content and trusting God to provide it. I recommit myself and relinquish the sermon back to God.

The Word of God and my own lived experience has taught me repeatedly that the way through is always communion with God. My first experience of preaching before a congregation left an indelible imprint on me. I had worked at preparing my debut sermon for weeks. I was very nervous. And though I had spoken countless times at church, this was Sunday morning, prime time, and there was clearly something different about preaching. But despite all of my efforts, I just couldn't bring the sermon together. On Saturday evening, the night before I was to preach, I sat in the center of my bed with my Bible and my notes spread all around me. I didn't know where to begin. I kept praying for God to order my thoughts, but that didn't happen. In anguish I prayed harder, but to no avail. And then I heard an internal voice: "Go take a shower." I railed, "No, I'll never get this done." But the voice persisted. Finally, I conceded. I took a shower.

As I reentered my bedroom, my first thought was "Now I can get to work on this sermon." But when I sat on my bed, in the midst of all my study materials, I heard the voice again: "Now, worship me." "Well," I thought, "this is ridiculous. How can I worship with a sermon hanging over my head?" I began to beseech and implore the Lord to please, please give me what to say. But again I heard, "Worship me." Exhausted and frustrated, perplexed and anxious, my only salvation was to give up all hope of ever having a sermon. I raised my arms in reluctant surrender to God. And as I lifted my hands in praise, something happened. The emotional turmoil that had seized me began to dissipate, like a fever. I felt lightness in that sacred moment. The sermon was no longer the focus. My anxiety gave way to praise and worship, and soon I was lost in adoration of God.

When I emerged from this experience, it dawned on me that I still didn't have a sermon. But the Spirit said, "Preach what you just experienced." "Okay," I said out loud, and I did. The title of the sermon was "O Come Let Us Adore Him." It was the Christmas Sunday sermon, and by the end of it, the entire congregation was on its feet, arms raised toward heaven, adoring God. God never gave me a manuscript, but through worship, God gave me the message. The congregation became privy to the intimate conversations that had taken place between God and myself as preacher.

Sometimes the sermon flows together, and sometimes it's a prolonged labor and difficult delivery. But no matter what, the worship of God and the return to a prayerful meditation of the text enable me to reconnect with God's presence and the spirit of the message. The pressure gives way as my energy is directed away from deadlines and toward a life-giving relationship with my first love. Through communion with God, I find my path once again and receive enough light by which to see. I begin slowly and methodically to build line upon line, working as long as needed to produce a draft by Thursday afternoon. But, there's still a lot of work to be done.

Some of this phase of sermon writing is the hardest work we do: letting go. I have to edit out things to which I was really attached. In this phase everything has to be fluid and up for grabs. I am praying that the Spirit will guide me in identifying what is most essential and what impedes the sermon; what stays and what goes. Then finally, having surrendered the sermon to God, I move into my Sabbath time.

On the fifth and sixth days, I rest. I pursue other avenues of healing and restoration. I do not focus on the sermon but am always open as the Spirit tugs on my sleeve with new thoughts. It is common for me to scribble down notes to myself even as I rest and recreate, as new insights surface during my Sabbath. I jot them down and tuck them away for future reference, and I am often surprised, relieved, and delighted to come upon these notes.

Early Sunday morning, when my new week begins, I am up and in my study once again, notes in hand. I commit myself and the sermon to God, and I ask for guidance. Pulling the sermon up on the computer, I integrate the changes that have come to me throughout the weekend. I comb through it several times, inserting last minute revisions. Typically, there is more elimination than integration of new material. Now I pray to be relieved of my perfectionism, to have the willingness to let go and let God, and then I head for the church.

From the call to worship until I stand in the pulpit to preach the Word, I am permeable and surrendering—relinquishing the rights to the sermon to God. I stand to preach, and the Word of God begins to go forth. It is never clearer than during and after it is preached, when I become aware of the rough places and the need to cut for the sake of timeliness, or to expound on certain points. I may suddenly remember a story or illustration that I wished I had included. Sometimes, there is still time to weave it into the fabric of my sermon, or maybe it has to wait until long after I have preached it. But in any case, the work of preparation—of prayer, of meditation, of study, of silence, of waiting, and of laboring in revision after revision, helps me to stand in the trust that I have done my best to capture and articulate for that Sunday the Word, the will, and the hope of my Lord.

Sermon: "Neckbone Faith"

VERONICA R. GOINES

Thus says the LORD:
Cursed are those who trust in mere mortals
    and make mere flesh their strength,
        whose hearts turn away from the LORD.
They shall be like a shrub in the desert,
    and shall not see when relief comes.
They shall live in the parched places of the wilderness,
    in an uninhabited salt land.
Blessed are those who trust in the LORD,
    whose trust is the LORD.
They shall be like a tree planted by water,
    sending out its roots by the stream.
It shall not fear when heat comes,
    and its leaves shall stay green;
in the year of drought it is not anxious,
    and it does not cease to bear fruit.

Jeremiah 17:5–10

He came down with them and stood on a level place, with a great crowd of his disciples and a great multitude of people from all Judea, Jerusalem, and the coast of Tyre and Sidon. They had come to hear him and to be healed of their diseases; and those who were troubled with unclean spirits were cured. And all in the crowd were trying to touch him, for power came out from him and healed all of them.

Then he looked up at his disciples and said:
    "Blessed are you who are poor,
        for yours is the kingdom of God.

"Blessed are you who are hungry now,
    for you will be filled.
"Blessed are you who weep now,
    for you will laugh.

"Blessed are you when people hate you, and when they exclude
you, revile you, and defame you on account of the Son of Man.
Rejoice on that day and leap for joy, for surely your reward is
great in heaven; for that is what their ancestors did to the
prophets.

"But woe to you who are rich,
    for you have received your consolation.
"Woe to you who are full now,
    for you will be hungry.
"Woe to you who are laughing now,
    for you will mourn and weep.

"Woe to you when all speak well of you, for that is what their
ancestors did to the false prophets."

Luke 6:17–26

When I was growing up, our extended family would gather after
church on Sunday afternoons for a traditional soul food meal
that my mother and aunts had prepared the night before. The
atmosphere within the house was thick with anticipation, and
the air was punctuated by the aroma of our favorite foods. But I
must admit that there was one food that always frustrated me,
and that was the neck bone. I'm sorry. I just never could understand why anyone would want to work that hard for protein. But
as I looked around at my parents and adult relatives and friends,
they all relished the experience of neck bones. They'd sit there
and root and suck on one a while, smacking and savoring the
moment. "Ummmmm" was the table conversation. And eventually, with a smile of deep satisfaction, they'd pull out a neck
bone, licked clean of any and all remnants of meat.

But my neck bone efforts were pitiful, because even when I
finished working on one, most of the meat was still on the bone.
I didn't have the gift of "neckboneology," the dedication and
desire to get into the nooks and crannies. And I still marvel this
time each year when we celebrate the culmination of black history month with our annual soul food feast. Folk line up at the
buffet table; "Oh please, give me one of those neck bones," they
say. And I think, "Here we go again."

But I have come to realize that neck bones are a metaphor for the experience of African Americans and for all people who, by grace, possess the faith to receive the scraps of this world and create a feast. Henri Nouwen, in *The Wounded Healer*, writes, "A Christian community is therefore a healing community, not because wounds are cured and pains are alleviated, but because wounds and pains become openings or occasions for a new vision."[3] Anyone can take a slab of ribs and make a filling meal. Anyone can make a feast of filet mignon. But a neck bone? Well, that's an occasion for a new vision. It is a vision of blessing.

And so, when given rags, the women formed quilting bees. When given ham bones, they fed whole communities. They sang, "Hambone, hambone, where you been; round the world and back again," because the hambone had been to every house on the block. From bits and pieces of pork and broth, hog head cheese was made; from the intestines of pigs, chittlins'; from the fields, wild greens; from cornmeal, hot-water corn-bread; and from neck bones came rich and savory stock in which to cook greens, black-eyed peas, soups, stuffing, stews, gravy, and much more. There was no end to the utility of neck bones. Through the common experience of suffering, in the depths of oppression and slavery, emerged a faith and generos-ity that was the source of life, joy, creativity, nourishment, com-munity, and blessing.

Because it was the custom of Africans to take on the deities of the new lands they entered, in time the slaves embraced the reli-gion of their slave masters. The slavers attempted to use the Christian religion to control the slaves. But when you use some-thing that has liberating power for the purpose of containing and controlling, you just need to know it won't work. Howard Thur-man tells the story of his grandmother, who was an ex-slave and a devout Christian. She never learned to read and depended on others to read to her. Thurman always wondered why she would only allow him to read the Psalms, Isaiah, and the Gospels, again and again, and from the Pauline Epistles, only First Corinthians 13. He finally garnered the courage to ask her why she was so selective in her Scripture choices. And she told him how her slave master controlled the slaves' exposure to the Word of God by enlisting white preachers to preach from the Epistles: "Slaves, obey your earthly masters . . . as you obey Christ" (Eph. 6:5). The preacher would promise that if the slaves were obedient, God would bless them. But although Thurman's grandmother could not read, she was adept at discerning the voice of God. With a deep love of Scripture, tempered by a wholesome suspicion, she engaged her neck bone faith in rooting around and plumbing this new-found theology to discover what was the authentic religion of Jesus.

The slave masters preemptively sought to oppress the slaves by denying them the right to read. Howard Thurman explained: "It was dangerous to let the slave understand that the life and teachings of Jesus meant freedom for the captive and release for those held in economic, social, and political bondage."[4] But slaves subverted their vile efforts by developing the gift of extemporaneous preaching in the sanctuary of the "invisible church," nestled in the woods, beneath the covering of moonlight. Here, they perfected the art of memorizing through attentive listening long passages of Scripture and delivering them in call and response to their congregations. Here, the spirituals emerged out of phrases from the sermon that resonated, that fed their souls.

The inability to read and write did not thwart the slaves' ability to communicate or receive the truth. Rather, the spirituals held significance and implications for deliverance in life on earth. Many of the songs contained coded messages, both spiritual and directional toward freedom in the North. In "O Canaan, sweet Canaan, I am bound for the land of Canaan," Canaan was the North. Every effort to restrain the slave was met by the creative resourcefulness of neck bone faith. Every attempt to foster dependence was surmounted by an increased dependence on God. The slaves had appropriated the message of Jeremiah 17. They learned to lean on the arm of God and not man. Divine liberation of the slave was the central theological concept of the spirituals. They facilitated a common and transcendent experience of worship—spontaneous and extemporaneous, born of Holy Spirit power and every deep human emotion, embodied memory and present reality.

Blacks were taught a faulty theology by white churches, which was that they were cursed. A curse is defined as an "alien voice that tells a lie about us, calls forth that lie, and leads to alienation."[5] If ever a people had a right to be depressed, the exiled children of Africa did. Peter D. Kramer discusses in his book *Against Depression* that the opposite of depression isn't happiness. The opposite of depression is resilience. It's not the absence of guilt and sadness, but is the ability to find a path away from those feelings.[6] The slaves would have been justified in looking down like the shrub in Jeremiah 17. It would have been understandable that they could not perceive the blessing amid such suffering. But for the descendants of Africa, the path away from depression and toward resilience was rooted, like a tree planted by the water, in the religion of Jesus; a religion that became, for them, what someone once called a precious bane.

Jesus teaches that it is crucial to learn to discern the voice of the curse from that of the blessing—to know the truth of one's identity. The white church tried to impart a passive, blonde-haired, blue-eyed, fair-skinned Jesus, but in time, slaves excavated the stories of Exodus, the Prophets, and the Gospels, and claimed a radical Savior. Like them, Jesus was poor, saying, "Foxes have holes and birds of the air have nests, but the Son of Man has no place to lay his head" (Matt 8:20). Like them, Jesus was a product of a minority group living within an oppressive dominant culture as a Jew in the Roman Empire. Jesus knew well their reality. This Jesus pronounces blessings upon the displaced and dispossessed peoples of all time, saying "blessed are you" (Luke 6:20b).

"A blessing is an external voice that speaks a word of truth about us that resonates deeply within us and calls forth that truth from within us to be manifested in the world."[7] Because Jesus sees the slaves, loves them, assures them that they will be cared for—through bread, through fish, through neck bones—their existence is affirmed. When their true identity is revealed and deeper self-understanding perceived, God's blessing and protection is revealed, too. As Luke's Gospel catches in its sweep Jew and Gentile, slave and free, male and female, the slaves are included in the kingdom. This authentic and liberating gospel allowed blacks to reclaim their blessedness and to embrace this paradoxical faith.

Neck bone faith reveals and confronts. In Luke 6, the words of Jesus are written in "performative language," meaning that by his very pronouncement of blessings and woes, Jesus overthrows the whole social and religious order. This is a Genesis moment, a moment of re-creation. Jesus says, in essence, "Let there be," (v. 20) and it is done! Jesus' words bring about a new reality. He speaks a new world into being. And for the Jewish religious elite, in the words of Walt Brueggemann, "The world for which they had been so carefully prepared was being taken away from them, by the grace of God."[8] Jesus preaches waking up to blessing, and in doing so, turns the world upside down.

Black people, working in the blistering, scorching, dehydrating sun of the South, had every reason to give up, to give out, and to give in, but they learned that to lean on the arm of God and discern the blessings of Jesus gave them a wealth that surpassed all understanding. The slaves found in Jesus Christ not an opiate for the people but a combustible for liberation. Like trees planted by the rivers of water they yielded the fruit of resilience and strength; as co-creators with God, they brought life out of chaos, light out of darkness, and hope out of despair.

You may have parents who survived the Holocaust or the Japanese internment camps of World War II. Maybe your great-grandparents lived through the horrors of slavery. Or perhaps you are a present-day refugee of the Sudan, Haiti, or Hurricane Katrina. You may be living with catastrophic illness. It takes an overcoming faith to bring you through such realities. Neck bone faith emerges out of dire circumstances, with power to transform those circumstances.

And because neck bone faith can do all that, come the last Sunday in February, I will stand in the buffet line at the soul food feast and say to the servers, "I'd like some neck bones, please." I will give thanks and give neck bones another try. I will savor and enjoy the experience. I will acknowledge my parents and ancestors, who taught me well how to hold to God's unchanging hand, to receive the scraps of this world and create a feast, to perceive the goodness of God in the midst of adversity, and to hear the blessings of Jesus above the curses of this world.

4

Rightly Dividing the Word

CYNTHIA L. HALE

I love to preach. I love the exhilaration of standing before the people of God while proclaiming his truth in ways that bring transformation and joy. I love the satisfaction one has in knowing that one has rightly divided the Word of God. Rightly dividing the Word takes preparation. Early in my preaching career, I learned the importance of preparing to preach by preparing myself as well as the text.

Preparing one's self involves spending intimate time with God through prayer, reading the Word, and solitude. Morning is my favorite time for prayer. Through the years, I have learned the secret of what I call *an early morning rendezvous with God*. I steal away to a big chair in my study or a corner of the sofa in the family room. It seems that God meets me there in a special way.

I have tried praying, studying, and preparing the sermon in my office at the church, but there are too many distractions, internal as well as external. Even when my office door is closed, I find myself thinking of a number of things that I need to ask my assistant or a staff person. At home, the only thing that competes for my attention is the telephone. Through the years, I have learned to ignore the rings or the press of other items that seek to distract me. It is important for me to deal with first things first and to keep the main thing *the main thing*. As the pastor and the primary preacher, preaching is my primary responsibility.

I begin my time with the Lord by reading a division of the Psalms and the text that I'm preaching that week, if it is already identified. I like to know what I am preaching early in the week. This is important to me because I like to live with the text for a week.

Living with the text allows me to become personal with it. If it is not personal—if the text does not speak to me and stir up something inside me—it will be very unlikely that I will be able to stir up anything in the folks to whom I am preaching it.

Allistair Begg says in the book *Great Preaching*:

> The first heart God's word need to reach is that of the preacher. There will be no benefit to our people from expository preaching unless we ourselves are being impacted by the Scripture we're preparing to preach. It is imperative, when we're dealing with the biblical text, that we're personally changed by this.

He then quotes John Owen on the power of truth in our own souls:

> A person only preaches a sermon well to others if he/she has first preached it to himself/herself. If he/she does not thrive on the food he/she prepares, he/she will not be skilled at making it appetizing for others. If the Word does not dwell in power in us, it will not pass in power from us.[1]

I also use devotional guides such as *A Guide to Prayer for Ministers and Other Servants* by Rueben P. Job and Norman Shawchuck.[2] I find that my devotional reading often providentially includes thoughts that help inform my preaching. Reading the newspaper as well as articles and books on a variety of subjects can also help prime the pump, making sermon preparation fluid as well as providing sermon introductory material and illustrations.

Preaching the Word of God is a serious task. As God's anointed, we are privileged to speak on behalf of God in an effort to change lives. It is through the foolishness of preaching that men and women are made aware of and convicted of sins and shown the way to be reconciled to God through Christ and given peace within. Through preaching, faith is developed. Listeners find in sermons the answers to life's difficult questions; they are taught precepts to live obediently, practical principles to live victoriously, and promises to live faithfully. Every time I preach, I preach for change in the lives of the people and in the world.

When I preach, I believe that the Word of God will not return empty but will accomplish the purpose for which God speaks it through me. This belief has encouraged me time and time again when my preaching has been met with empty stares, when it felt like I was making no impact at all, or when I was clear that I had flunked.

Every preacher has felt a sense of failure at some time or another and wondered whether she or he would ever preach again. As a pastor of a church, I quickly discovered that I would have another chance to preach and the congregation would be waiting to hear. I worried needlessly about flunking until I read Hannah Whitall Smith's comments in *The Christian's Secret of a Happy Life.*

> Never indulge, at the close. . . . This has been of unspeakable value to me. When the temptation comes, as it mostly does to every worker after a performance of any service, to indulge in these reflections, either of one sort or the other, I turn from them at once and positively refuse to think about my work at all, leaving it with the Lord to overrule the mistakes, and to bless it as He chooses. I believe there would be fewer "blue Mondays" for ministers of the Gospel than there are now if they would adopt this plan; and I am sure all workers would find their work less wearing.[3]

My most memorable sermon to date is the one I preached on Valentine's Day. It was titled "Whatever Happened to Black Love?" and referred to the Song of Solomon, about the joys of marital love that is affectionate, appreciative, and affirming. This sermon spoke profoundly and practically about intimate relationships, and I felt free and passionate about what I was preaching. The people were right there with me throughout the entire sermon; it felt like they were in the palm of my hand. The next night we had a couple's event, and a record number of couples attended and joined the ministry. Not all my sermons, however, have had such an impact or positive response. For example, one New Year's Eve, I preached a sermon about "forgetting what is behind and pressing towards what is ahead" from Phil. 2:12–14. Though the sermon was well prepared and biblically sound, I failed to answer the question "So what?" As I preached, the people were flat and not long into the preaching moment. I lost my passion. I couldn't wait for the sermon to be over.

I must admit that through the years, I have struggled with being influenced by the response of the people during my preaching. As a Disciple of Christ, I was raised in a church where there was no call and response. Most of the preachers I heard growing up were very intellectual and informational, but there was little inspiration. Though I was exposed to a variety of preaching in seminary, by that time my style had been shaped.

Alvin O. Jackson, my pastor while in seminary, said, "Preaching is caught rather than taught." While I believe that persons can be taught the fundamentals and principles of preaching, one's style is formed by the preachers one hears. As I started to preach in a black church context, I wasn't sure I could "pull it." I was insecure with my style of preaching for years, thinking that the people wanted to hear a more celebrative preaching, particularly at the end. If people didn't respond to my preaching, I felt like I had not been successful.

One day, a close friend said to me, "No one can beat you being you. You have something unique to offer in your preaching and ministry that no one else can give. The people who come to hear you preach come because they want to hear you and what you have to share, the way you share it." Through the years, I have found my own voice and become comfortable with who I am as a preacher. An experienced preacher once told me that when you preach, you need to ask whether or not you have spoken to where the people live, move, and have their being. I remember that New Year's Eve message was a great Bible lesson, but I am not sure if the people understood after hearing it what a difference it could make in their lives.

When preparing a sermon, I am concerned about making sure that what I am saying speaks to the listening congregation. It is important to be relevant. I ask God to show me what he would have me say to the people and what they need to hear. I also spend time listening to people—to their issues, concerns, questions, and struggles. Sometimes as I write I see the faces of specific people who I know have a particular need, or the Holy Spirit brings them to mind. I imagine our having a conversation, and am particularly blessed when someone says to me later, "You read my mind"; "How did you know?"; "Were you in my house last night?"; "I needed to hear that sermon." That helps me to know that I am listening to God and connecting with the people.

Selecting *what* to preach has been an interesting experience for me through the years. I was introduced to preaching from the Common Lectionary in seminary, but I quickly rejected that approach, saying that I needed to be led by the Holy Spirit in my selection of texts. What I discovered after a couple of years of preaching was that I needed a systematic method by which to choose my texts under the leadership of the Holy Spirit. Otherwise I found myself preaching my favorite texts and themes, being redundant and not addressing many issues that needed to be addressed.

When I became a pastor, I was a thematic preacher for the most part, developing my sermons around a yearly theme that helped to focus the life and ministry of our church. I have found this approach to be very effective, particularly as I developed a young congregation of persons new to a relationship with God and with the church. I read somewhere that you have to preach where you want people to go. Therefore, as I sought to disciple and teach the people the essentials of being a Christian and a member of the church, I preached sermon series and texts on spiritual growth and development, discipleship, evangelism, giving, discovering and employing one's gifts, and so on.

Informed by the needs of the people and the world in which we live, I found myself becoming more issue oriented in my preaching, speaking both to personal issues and the issues that we face in the world. Today, I find myself preaching more prophetically to bring hope and healing, peace and justice, in an effort to motivate the listeners to influence and transform this present world into the kingdom of God. I believe I have found a sweet balance in what I preach.

My preaching style is primarily expositional. I love to walk through the Scriptures as I preach a series of sermons on a theme or preach through a book of the Bible. As I said earlier, I like to identify my text early in the week and read through it as a part of my devotions. By Thursday evening, I am ready to do my exegetical work on the text. My process with the text is as follows:

Having lived with the text for a week, I then write it down in a notebook, underlining or circling key words and phrases that I want to research. Sometimes at this point I will begin to outline the sermon, identifying key points. I love alliteration and identifying key points that surface from the text with phrases or words that begin with the same letter or words. It is at this point that I may brainstorm, jotting down some thoughts, images, and illustrations. Next, I do my word study. Through the years, I have used a variety of reference books and commentaries, some of which are listed in the bibliography at the end of this essay. Recently, I purchased the Libronix Library that contains these references and more.

Whenever I am preaching thematic or issue-oriented sermons, I read books, articles in the paper, and magazines, and I search the Internet on the subject. It is important for me to be as well versed on the subject as possible. I like to do all my reading, research, and study one day and then start writing the next. I find that when I sleep on it or let it percolate awhile, writing is easier. There are times when I go to bed not quite sure where I'm going, or what my introduction or closing will be. But when I wake up in the morning, everything has come together; the outline is rolling around in my head, and I can't wait to write the sermon down and deliver it.

Finding examples is the hardest part of sermon preparation for me. I envy persons who seem to perceive an illustration in almost every movie they see, book they read, and conversation they have. I find most of my illustrations in my own life experiences or the experiences of others. I am very transparent, sharing my joys and sorrows, strengths and weaknesses. Occasionally, I will see an illustration that speaks to me and will write it down for future reference. I also retell stories that I've heard someone else tell, giving them credit of course.

The most important part of a sermon for me is the introduction. I try to begin every sermon in a personal way, with a line out of the life stories of the people to whom I am preaching. I may ask a question or state a concern that I know people are struggling with in their personal lives or in the world at large. I want to grab their attention, hook them early, and build their interest as I proceed. My sermons are always spoken from the third person plural. I say "we" because I am having a dialogue with the people I'm addressing and want to convey that we are in this together.

When I preach, I celebrate all the way through. I preach with joy and with passion. I have heard Henry Mitchell say on occasion that folks will do what they celebrate. We have to help people understand that there is joy in living for Jesus and in serving the Lord, and that the joy of the Lord is our strength. This joy is the means by which we handle the challenges and circumstances of life, gaining victory over them. It is with joy that we are to manage the affairs of life at home, work, and school, and with joy we are to make a difference in our world. The life that we live in Christ is to be lived with joy, and it is through the foolishness of preaching that we teach persons how to do this despite the many circumstances in their lives that militate against having joy.

I told you earlier that I was raised in a Disciples of Christ church where most of the preaching I heard growing up was an intellectual discourse, speaking more to the head than to the heart, providing more information than inspiration. This is the way I started preaching, but what I later discovered was that while the sharing of information is good and it is needed, one must balance the information in preaching with inspiration. Real change or transformation in a person's life comes when there is a connection between the head and the heart of the preacher and the listener. Real change is not simply an intellectual process; it is an experiential and emotional one as well. The people of God not only need to hear the words we speak, but as the young people say today, they need to "feel" you. The people who listen to us need to feel the power and the passion of the words we speak. R. E. O. White tells us in *A Guide to Preaching*,

> Nothing moves the will but emotion. The word emotion simply means "that which moves." To cultivate emotionalism for its own sake is indeed superficial, immature, even dangerous in some cases. But to despise emotion, and to avoid it, is to condemn all preaching to sterile ineffectiveness.[4]

Preaching with passion and celebrating all the way through, I often end my sermons with a story or illustration that brings it all together, or I end by summarizing the practical principles for living that I just preached. Sometimes I close with people having to contemplate or make a decision about what they have just heard. I am a full-manuscript preacher. In other words, I write a full manuscript every time I preach, but it depends on my level of comfort in the service as to whether or not I stick to the manuscript. There are times when I never even look at it. Other times, I will read it word for word. I find that I engage the people more when I don't stand at the podium and read the manuscript but move freely through the congregation or across the pulpit area.

Generally from Sunday to Sunday, I employ the same sermonic form, but there are times when in an effort to be creative, I will use another form. One Sunday, I introduced my sermon with a movie clip; another time I did a PowerPoint presentation. There have been times when I used a story to present the message. It is important to me to be fresh and relevant and to connect with the people. As I said earlier, I like to explore different ways of doing so. As one who is invited to do a lot of conferences and special events, I have through the years written new sermons in keeping with whatever theme I was given. Having preached for thirty years now, I have a reservoir of sermons to choose from on most subjects. I enjoy not having to create a new sermon every time I preach, and I love preaching some of my sermons again. As a pastor, I find that when I go to different churches, the people there are the same. The messages that God has given me for Ray of Hope speak just as powerfully to another congregation, just as the letters Paul wrote to the saints in Corinth, Ephesus, and Rome speak to us today.

Staying fresh and preaching relevant messages to the same congregation week in and week out is a challenge. I am now in my twenty-second year, and I am amazed that there are people who have been listening to me for that long and still want to hear me. The way I stay fresh and relevant is through my connection with God and with the people, through reading and living in the world. I embrace life to the fullest. I know what is going on. I live among the people, and I expose myself to many and varied life settings and social and cultural experiences so that I can stay on the cutting edge of my craft. There are times, however when no matter what you do, it feels like the heavens are shut up tight! You as the preacher are asking, "Is there no Word from the Lord?" Your soul is dry and empty, and you have nothing to say to the people. In these times, I will say to friends, "I have nothing to say!"

There is always a Word from the Lord whether we feel it or not. I preach through the dry periods like I preach through a storm, studying and praying as usual, making an effort to write, even when it takes much longer. God is faithful! He always comes through. It is in these times that I am reminded that I'm not the real preacher: he is! I am the instrument that he uses to communicate what he wants to say to his people through me.

BIBLIOGRAPHY

Barclay, William. *The Daily Study Bible Series—New Testament*. Philadelphia: The Westminster Press, 1958.

Gaebelein, Frank E. *The Exposition's Bible Commentary*. Grand Rapids: Zondervan Publishing House, 1981.

Gibson, C. L. *The Daily Study Bible Series—Old Testament*. Philadelphia: The Westminster Press and Edinburgh: The Saint Andrew Press, 1982.

Job, Rueben P. and Norman Showchuck. *A Guide to Prayer for Ministers and Other Servants*. Nashville: The Upper Room, 1983.

Smith, Hannah Whitall. *The Christian's Secret of a Happy Life*. Fleming H. Reid.

Strong, John. *The Exhaustive Concordance of the Bible*. Nashville: Abingdon, 1975.

Tenney, Merrill C. *The Pictorial Dictionary of the Bible*. Nashville: The Southwestern Company.

Unger, Merrill F. *The New Unger's Bible Dictionary*. Chicago: Moody Press, 1988.

Vine, W. E. *An Expository Dictionary of New Testament Words*. Nashville: Thomas Nelson Publishers, 1952.

Wiersbe, Warren. *The Bible Exposition Commentary*. Wheaton, IL: Victor Books, 1989.

Sermon: "Whatever Happened to Black Love?" Song of Songs 1:1–5, 9–15

CYNTHIA L. HALE

It's the season of love, the time when we celebrate what the Greeks call *eros*, the intense passionate kind of love that people enjoy when they are so enamored with the other that nothing else matters. I want to talk with you about black love. Black love is a powerful and passionate love that is intense and irresistible, like the people who give it its unique flavor. As African Americans, we are a strong people, and our love is strong. There is no question that we are passionate! Our emotions are intense and expressive in the way that we interact with one another and life. Our laughter is loud and lyrical. Our anger is hot and sometimes uncontrollable. When we are happy, we shout; when we hurt, we cry; when we party, we party hard. Our feelings are expansive and exhaustive, and so is our love. We have this ability to love and keep on loving, or at least we used to love that way.

Whatever happened to black love? we must ask ourselves, as affairs run rampant and 50 percent of marriages end in divorce. Where did our love go? Don't those of you who consummated your love in commitment and marriage expect it to last forever? Everyone knows that human love is elusive; it is fleeting. Human love is often based on feelings, and feelings come and go. Human love is fragile, easily injured. An unkind word spoken in a fit of anger or carelessly takes root in the receiver's heart, and when it is not quickly removed through apology and forgiveness, it festers and threatens permanent damage to the relationship.

Love is easily injured, especially when it is taken for granted. We take our relationships for granted when we assume that our relationships are solid and do not need to be nurtured, cared for, affirmed, and supported. Relationships have to be stoked daily like a fire to keep them hot. Women and men share appreciable differences that require understanding and sensitivity. Each has different needs that we expect to be met in marriage: such as the need for sexual fulfillment, affection, admiration, conversation, support, and honesty. We cannot assume that the other knows and understands what our needs are. Therefore, we must communicate.

In marriage, what began as a wonderful affair between two persons committed to work together, struggle together, and stay together until death do us part can quickly dissolve in the face of increasing debts and decreasing funds. The demands placed on us from day to day cause stress and fatigue and leave us longing for space and a place to cool out when we get home without having to deal with more demands and hassles. The fact that children, though wonderful, take up more time and energy than imagined or planned for can cause feelings of neglect and frustration to surface over not having enough intimate time to spend with one another, privately without interruptions or distractions. Growing older, folks can get set in their ways and lose the knack for creativity in the loving of one another and can allow the fire to go out.

All these things and more can cause what is already elusive to take wings and to raise the question, What is happening to our love, the love we shared? How does one regain the joy of it all? Does the excitement of being in relationship have to end? As an eternal optimist and one who is hopelessly in love with love, I believe the love that two lovers share, the excitement of being in a wonderfully intimate relationship, never has to end, even when dealing with the cold harsh realities of living from day to day. Therefore, I lift up for your consideration this morning a powerful little book for lovers in the Bible, the Song of Songs or the Song of Solomon. Readers of the Song of Solomon are initially astonished to find such sexually provocative sayings and images in the Bible, but how quickly we forget that the Bible is a book about life, seeking to keep it real by speaking to and about real-life situations, needs, and desires. The Song of Songs is a book about love, love that is divine and love that is human. It is a book on the praise of love and God, who is the source of all love, human and divine, spiritual and sexual.

Love is what God had in mind when he created humans for relationships both with God's self and with one another. The relationship that God established, the oneness that God was ordaining for husbands and wives, is to be a love that is both spiritual and sexual. Our sexuality is a gift of God. It is a good gift. When God created us in his image and likeness for relationships with one another, he intended for men and women to enjoy one another in marriage physically as well as emotionally. The Song of Songs is a powerfully dramatic, poetic depiction of love between a woman and a man and of what marriage should be about, with its passion, frankness, openness, tenderness and bold expressions of affection and desire.

It is written as a play. The voice of the lover is most likely that of King Solomon and his beloved bride. Their friends serve as the chorus, perhaps to show the importance of positive relationships outside of marriage that affirm marital relationships. In the dialogue that takes place are spelled out vital components of love that will make a relationship between a man and a woman all that it should be. The dialogue is mutual though it begins with the woman speaking. She is free to initiate the dialogue and express her love, but at no time should it be assumed that the conversation and the commitment are one-sided, because her lover is as vocal as she is. Communication is the foundation of any relationship, and especially marriage. One of the needs that women have is to have their men talk to them. Women need to be asked about their day and then be listened to as they give details—even after a long day, brothers. When you come home tired, just know that it is important if you want to please your wife and keep her happy to take a little time to talk.

In this love poem the sister begins by speaking of her desire for her lover's affection (1:1). Love is affectionate. Lovers delight in one another and long for each other. If your love has grown cold, guess why! Perhaps you've gotten too accustomed to each other. You assume the other knows how you feel, so you don't have to say it or show it; he or she already knows. How will your partner know if you don't communicate; if you are not willing to show it? Women need affection; men need sexual fulfillment. But you can't have one without the other. Can you imagine what kind of relationship you would have if both of you got busy giving the other what the other needs? Some folks have become comfortable and allowed their relationships to become stale, and so you need to always find creative ways to express your love and affection for one another. Don't use the children as an excuse for not being affectionate to one another. It's crazy, but we let our children see us fuss with one another but not kiss.

One of the fondest memories of my childhood was watching my parents show affection to one another. Whenever one of their favorite songs came on the radio or record player, they danced. When was the last time you showed your beloved how much you care? Love is affectionate. Love appreciates the other and the relationship. In Song 1:9 the lover speaks, comparing his beloved to a beautiful mare. In modern language, comparing your beloved to a horse does not sound very exciting. But at the time of this writing, a mare was a thing of rare beauty. The brother was paying the ultimate compliment to her sexual attraction, accented by her jewelry, and he would provide her with earrings of gold, studded with silver to further enhance her beauty. No occasion is noted; it is a gift just because. He refers to her as "my darling," a key word because it comes from the root word translated *amica*, which means companion or friend. It is a word with a strong connotation of commitment and desire.

Love appreciates the other as lover and friend. It does not focus on one over the other. There is a sensitive balance between the two. One cannot truly be your lover in the fullest sense if he or she is not your friend. Friendship is so important between husbands and wives. When you are friends, you can talk about anything. When you are friends, you enjoy doing things together. You look for ways to enhance one another's lives. Friendship enhances our love for one another. Love is appreciative of who a person is and what he or she does for us. Love says thank you for dinner, for picking up the children, for changing the oil, for washing the car, for washing the clothes, for just being there. It is just nice being appreciated even for the routine responsibilities. Love doesn't let anything go unnoticed. Love is affectionate; love appreciates and love affirms.

Finally, there is a wonderful exchange of affirmation between the two. Love is affirming. When you are affirming one another, it is important to be specific about what you like about the other, what turns you on about them, what it is that causes the other to stand out, to be unique. In a world where black men are constantly being torn down and sisters are dogged on videos, we need to be affirming of one another. Love is edifying; it builds one another up and does not tear down. Love is affectionate; love is appreciative; loves is affirming; love always hopes, always trusts, always perseveres; love never fails.

5

Preaching: A Holy and Human Venture

C. E. MCLAIN

Preparing and delivering the sermon is one of the many hats a pastor wears. We may, however, be called on to inspire others when our own personal inspiration is not immediately at hand. I have spent more than four decades as a preacher/pastor, so what follows are but mere snapshots of my preparation method. Usually the seasoned preacher settles in as an expository preacher or topical preacher and rarely deviates from this pattern, so for me every sermon should have a scriptural text and subject. One of the most difficult problems might be simply finding a comfortable beginning.

Getting an idea is a good place to start. fortunately, ideas for the preacher are not hard to find or receive; they are all around us, begging to be used. But first, prayer is essential because prayer helps prepare the preacher to receive and deliver the message of God. The late Dr. D. E. King suggested years ago that preaching is but an overage of the preacher's prayer life. Talking and listening to God has to be a part of the preachers' daily routine. When preparing the sermon, while at prayer, I always pray for the hearers. I pray that the Spirit will make their hearts fertile ground for the good seed of God's word.

Getting a sermon idea early in the week will prevent anxiety and make the preaching experience more meaningful to the preacher and the hearers. For the Sunday sermon, getting your idea Monday or earlier gives a week or longer to muse and write and then muse some more. Preachers must be constant seekers of ideas for sermons to teach, inspire, and guide their members and others. Whenever we run short or out of ideas, we can look at God's ideas. We are taught to think his thoughts after him. The bound book we call the Bible may be humankind's idea, but the Word is God's idea. The piano, organ, and other instruments used in worship may be humankind's ideas, but music is God's idea. Heaven, earth, men, women, children, all family members, the church, preaching, preachers, community members, compassion, forgiving, salvation, and giving are all God's ideas. The order of creation, day and night, the seasons, and the inevitable creation of humankind are all God's ideas. Good Friday and Easter morning were God's ideas also.

We can get ideas or new approaches to old ideas from our reading habits. Reading regularly is essential to fresh approaches to the sermon idea. *Be sure you know your Scripture.* The text is always the best part of the sermon. The late N. S. Brown of Houston, Texas, believed that church people are usually very forgiving. He insisted that church people in our culture would forgive the preacher for almost anything. The hearers will forgive the preacher for not speaking correct English. Preachers will likely be forgiven if they cannot parse pronouns or conjugate verbs. Their poor pulpit attire may also be forgiven.

But the hearers will not forgive a preacher who does not know the Scriptures. A misquote of the Scriptures is an abomination of imparting the inspired Word of God without a clear knowledge of the content of thought that has been given to humans. Reading the Scriptures must be a daily practice. I have found that it is not the quantity of reading but the quality of one's reading that is important. In addition to reading the Scriptures daily, other reading is essential. More than one good daily newspaper, a weekly reputable and national magazine, inspirational books on the subject, monthly periodicals, musicals, and some songs all help develop ideas. The dailies are helpful in keeping the mind abreast and fresh on events on the world stage as well as on the local scene.

Even though the preacher may have prepared a home-run, bases-clearing sermon for the coming worship, a sudden and unexpected national tragedy (e.g., the death of the president or governor), a declaration of war or other national disaster, or a tragedy within the congregation may well dictate a postponement of the planned sermon. In these circumstances the preacher will want to be sure to console the congregation mindfully and speak from the heart about the event. Any occurrence that involves a member or member family should be followed with a visit.

The preacher needs the preparation, latitude, mental integrity, and interest to read everything from Plato to *Playboy*. Stories and articles may be found in New Age or Generation X magazines that can be surprisingly informative. Novels are another great source of inspiration and relaxation. Many preachers enjoy novels so much they read continuously. When one novel has been read, another is immediately started. Og Mandino's *The Christ Commission* has been read by hundreds of thousands of ministers and parishioners. Olive Schrinner's *Track to The Water's Edge* is a rare find but worth the time to locate.

Slices of personal history can be found in the writings of fellow pastors. I heard about *Ashes for Breakfast* by Thomas J. Holmes several years before I finally located it. The story of a white southern pastor who tried to honor his church's foreign mission effort, only to be fired, is insightful. The pastor decided to stand alone when he accepted an African exchange student against the wishes and vote of his officers and church. The incident took place during the nineteen sixties at a church in Macon, Georgia, where the African exchange student came to worship Sunday after Sunday. But he was turned away each time. The church was located near the university campus where the student was studying, and when he was asked why he continued to come to the church, the student replied, "I was doing well in my own country with my own religion when missionaries from America found me and told me Jesus loved me. I believed them so much that I decided to study in America and visit one of his churches near my school. Apparently, the people at the church didn't love me as much as Jesus did."

Autobiographies are good sources for ideas and inspiration. Howard Thurman's *Life With Head and Heart* is as interesting reading now as it was when I read it twenty years ago. Newspapers, editorial pages, and magazines should be read regularly as well. I read the first few pages of the newspaper before reading the rest of the headlines and articles in the other sections to see if there is something that interests me. The Internet also aids in the research of ideas.

Observing nature is another way of keeping the homiletical eyeglasses clear. I walk everyday. I enjoy walking and reading and have practiced this routine for thirty-five years. I also walk outside in my neighborhood rather than use a treadmill. Once, while walking in the spring I came upon two butterflies. One was a pale lime green and the other was a multicolored, wide-winged creature. The lime-green butterfly was smaller and kept close to the ground. The multicolored butterfly seemed to catch the air current and elevated several feet above my head. With orange stripes on a black surface bordered by yellow, it moved up and down, barely flapping its wings. Soon it was out of sight.

The pale-green butterfly stopped between flights and rested on the grass for a few seconds before lifting off again. When I returned to my study, I researched everything I could on butterflies. I discovered that the harder the struggle for the caterpillar to get free from the cocoon, the stronger the wings and more beautiful the color. I realized that for the butterfly, beauty and strength come from a struggle. Also, I realized of the butterfly who was leaving that unsightly cocoon that little struggle usually means less beauty and strength.

The observation of people is another source for ideas. African Americans and other people of darker hue have broader noses and darker skin because our ancestors settled near the equator. Where the climate is hottest, breathing freely is crucial. Thus, our noses are broader. Also, the sun would fry the brain if the hair were not a certain kind. Sufficient melanin is needed as protection from the rays of the sun. All races are given anatomical structures and features to survive their environments. Anglos, settling in the colder climates, were given skin not too sensitive to cold and thin noses so their lungs would not freeze over. All of us are wonderfully and fearfully made.

Next, it is important to give ideas and thoughts time to ferment. There have been times when one idea was left to ferment in my mind while I worked on another idea that needed to be completed sooner. Critiquing one's own ideas helps in the pursuit of objectivity. Ideas are improved when they are in agitation in the preacher's own mind. Allowing an idea to argue with or question the preacher should not disturb or frighten the preacher into abandoning that thought. Once a text is chosen I begin to isolate the main thought and passage of Scripture. I contemplate inspiration to grow to the realization of something that must be developed fully.

Prepare for the occasion. The preacher should know the audience to be addressed, and the sermon should fit both the audience and the occasion. A Founder's day sermon, for example, will be different from one on stewardship. When preparing the sermon for a congregation, the preacher should be mindful of the church's annual calendar as well as the national calendar. For example, most African American congregations observe in some great or small fashion Martin Luther King Day. During the Christmas month of December, I usually preach sermons relative to the nativity. For example, there is the dark side of Christmas, the first one and our modern ones. The slave preacher seldom, if ever, ended a sermon without a reference to the crucifixion and the resurrection of Christ. If a preacher is invited to preach a doctrinal sermon, that is what should be planned and delivered.

The preacher should also be firmly aware of the amount of time that exists for guest appearances. When invited to preach in a pulpit not my own I ask my host how much time is allowed for the sermon and what time the worship is usually over. The average adult's attention span is approximately twenty minutes.

Once the preacher has decided on the idea and devoted time to examine it, it is time to zoom in on the dominant thought, word, Scripture, and resources. I believe in myself and in my divine calling to preach. Therefore, I allow my creative juices to have full flow. My effort is to let my creative thought processes produce as much of the text from personal ideas before I go on to other sources. References from commentaries, dictionaries, and other biblical sources are consulted, but not at the expense of my own imagination. Once I have given time to muse and mull over the idea and the Scripture, I always consult at least two other sources and, as John Bigsanio of Houston, Texas said years ago, "They are usually right."

When I enter the study of another pastor/preacher, I first observe their library. One can tell the reading habits of a preacher by the volumes on the shelves. If the only books on the shelves are commentaries, I immediately realize that there may be little reading done in the study as a part of the routine of the sermon preparation. I maintain a current set of commentaries that consist of helpful exegetical ideas on the Old and New Testaments. Over the years I have amassed many different Bibles of varying translations. I also keep two current and exhaustive dictionaries and at least one current thesaurus nearby.

Leading up to the day of finalizing the written sermon, I apply the Macleod and Becklehymer methods. Dr. Donald Macleod, retired professor of preaching at Princeton, advised his students to keep a pen and paper near at all times. This is helpful to the young preacher. A pad and pen can be kept on the lampstand by the bed. When I was younger, I would sit up in bed in the dark, reach for the light, and write down an idea or a Scripture to be remembered or looked up. Even today I find myself doing this several times during the night.

Dr. Macleod's approach to preaching was systemic. He emphasized that one should be thorough in one's preparation. Make the sermon interesting to the person on the street; keep the language simple and understandable, he admonished. Gary Eberble, chairman of the English

Department at Aquinas College in Grand Rapids, writes in his book *Dangerous Words*, "Language is not perfect by any means, but it is by far the best method we have to move ourselves forward, to figure our way out of our problems and to articulate our human condition."

Dr. Macleod also suggested using the five-inch index box for filing news articles and page numbers of lengthy quotes in books alphabetically. I have found this helpful especially in the early days of my preaching. Certain practices stay with the preacher.

Dr. Hunter Becklehymer, former professor of homiletics at Brite Divinity School, strongly suggested that the preacher set aside a whole day to complete the written draft of the sermon. Friday is the day I set aside to complete my manuscript. Saturday is a day of meditation. Sunday is a day of presentation. Monday is a day of recreation. Tuesday is a day of administration. Wednesday is a day of visitation. Thursday is a day of consultation. And Friday we begin again. However, the idea also remains in my thoughts, sometimes requiring quick pauses to stop and jot down a thought. Nights often involve an additional one or two hours of work when necessary.

During the time of preparing the manuscript all of the notes and quotes are kept near as I attempt to craft the introduction. The introduction is a brief capsule of the message to follow, and within it is a compact statement of what the hearer can expect. Also, a summary of the Scripture used is addressed. If it is easier to use a story to convey the ideas to follow or give the hearer an idea of the direction of the presentation, I will use it. For example, in a sermon based on Genesis 32 about Jacob meeting God on the run, I emphasize that Jacob was really running from himself. G. K. Chesterton, the English lay theologian of years past, tells the story of an architect that went to work every day by way of the same route. His problem was that each day he passed what he thought was the ugliest house he had ever seen. He saw it twice a day. Because the architect dealt with designing structures of beauty, he hated this house with a passion. It was so displeasing in appearance, and he hated it so much that he bought it and moved in so that he would not have to look at it. Many people have a Jacob present within themselves. It is a part of themselves they do not like and would rather not see, so they lose themselves within themselves to avoid looking at that part of their character that they despise so much.

After developing the idea or thought and keeping it in the front parlor of the mind, preachers have to let the idea capture and hold them. In our cultural vernacular, the pegs will come next. The pegs or points of the sermon will come from the text, and each enumerated point should make a complete sentence. I attempt to make the statement of each point as brief as possible without compromising the idea I seek to convey. Sometimes the preacher can use different words to introduce the point—for example, "First I'd like to say . . ." or "Next I would say. . . ." I have discovered that the idea may be retained easier when it is stated in a complete but succinct sentence.

The points or pegs give the sermon structure. They also help keep me conscious of time. When points are used, the preacher can develop an easy flow into the message and transition from the first point to the next. Using points can help in many ways. For example, using points can help keep the preacher focused, and points can help one gauge the time it will take to deliver the sermon.

One can also look at the points and make sure the use of Scripture has been correctly embraced to make the sermon help the hearers see themselves in the Bible. Illustrations, or word pictures, can be employed to help the listeners see themselves in the Scripture or in the message being conveyed. Many years ago I read Charles Reynolds Brown's *The Art of Preaching*. Dr. Brown suggested that the basis for the sermon is the Scripture and "the expository sermon will come from the more extended and systematic interpretation of a larger portion of Scripture." Addressing this larger portion of Scripture can be done in the body of the sermon, which I choose to divide into three or four points.

Within the points the preacher can bring to bear the "oaks and elms of good material" upon the sermon. In the first draft of the sermon jot down every good thought, even the mere underbrush in the forest of thought and imagination. They may grow as you continue to work. I adopted the practice of reading at least two newspaper comic strips a day. I also enjoy trivia. Then I read quotes of well-known and unknown individuals. In my preparation time I often regurgitate this material. It is like an agriculturist said of the chicken. The chicken eats everything, things that are nice and clean and things that are not. The chicken eats corn and seed, bugs and worms, scraps from the table, gravel, dirt, and odds and ends. The chicken eats anything it can swallow. And it all reappears in the general makeup of the hen as light and dark meat and good fresh eggs. This is also the place in the sermon to remember the sages and great theologians. Read them and listen to them if they can be located. Be sure to quote them accurately.

Points also help with organization and structure. The preacher does not want to be guilty of rambling and searching for the next thought or trying to figure out how it might support the thought that preceded it. Points also help me stay within a certain time frame. After writing manuscripts for the past years I know how much time it takes to deliver a certain amount of material.

Points make a sermon easier to preach. You can underscore, highlight, type, or write in bold letters those things that you really do not want to miss. In addition, the delivery of the written sermon divided into points will require less physical and mental energy on the part of the preacher and generate less anxiety compared to preaching without a written script. Finally, the written sermon divided into points enables the preacher to rework a sermon if necessary and repreach it over and over again.

Once the first draft has been written, I read, edit, spell-check, and check Scripture chapter and verse. I usually work from two sheets of paper at the same time, looking at the first while rewriting on the second sheet. Sometimes ideas will come in a downpour, and at other times ideas come slowly. I make it a practice of taking breaks during the preparation of the sermon and find that a break after every hour and a half or two can keep me fresh. A thirty-minute break, for example, can be very refreshing. I also have taken extended breaks from the preparation of the sermon when I come to the last point or the conclusion. Whether one is preaching with a manuscript or without a manuscript, one's physical and spiritual content must be equal with the content of the message.

Once the sermon has been crafted into the final draft I read it several times. I do not, however, attempt to memorize the sermon word for word. Instead, my goal is to become extremely familiar with the content. I remember where every part of the sermon is and know what is contained in the introduction, the points, and the conclusion.

When I know I have a good feel for the sermon I will think about it and challenge myself to see how familiar I am with the content. Going over the major themes in the introduction will come first because the conclusion is the easiest part for me to remember. Then I mentally review the main headings of the points. Finally, I make sure I am very familiar with the Scripture. I recite it openly and then reread the text to make sure I have a good grasp of its contents.

My father, who preached and pastored for more than fifty years, taught that a preacher should ride well, wear well, and rest well. Little will be gained if a preacher has labored in the study for hours and then is too exhausted to deliver the sermon. I set a time for myself for winding down and bringing the day of preparation to an end, and I give myself time to get up, get dressed, and be on time at the assigned place to preach on the day the sermon is to be delivered.

Another practice I have kept for many years is keeping a diary of sermons. I list the title, the date, and the place the sermon was preached. This information helps, especially in series preaching, revivals, and seminars, to prevent my being repetitious. The effective sermon is well prepared, structurally produced, thoroughly contemplated and absorbed, and seriously proscribed with God's guidance throughout the process of giving the Word of God to a God-fearer, a weak congregation, or a lonely soul.

Preachers should know their sermons. There are some disadvantages, in my opinion, to preaching with a manuscript and some definite advantages to preaching without one. As one who preaches without a manuscript, I find that I am left to incorporate new revelations into the presentation as I make my case. Lawyers, actors, and many others bring no script when they make their final presentations. Preaching without a script enables me to maintain eye contact with the people with whom I am attempting to communicate. Therefore, I can see whether there is an amen on their faces even if there is not one in their mouths.

For me, speaking without a manuscript came after many years. I have been blessed with a good memory. But I sometimes suffer from panic attacks, which can be violent and sometimes come with little warning. Knowing they lurk in the shadows of my emotions, however, I have learned to control them. I do not exert much energy or engage in too much conversation before I preach, and I never enter the pulpit or speaking place without a serious talk with "The Boss." He has not failed me. Though judging one's effectiveness as a preacher can be difficult and at times I have felt I might have missed the mark, often during the invitation or after the worship I have experienced times when numerous decisions for Christ were made or expressions of appreciation given.

In the African American culture, the sermon is not just a religious speech given to an assembled group by a clergyperson. The sermon is God's Word communicated to his people through human personality. Preaching should always be the main course, the centerpiece, and the main event in Christian worship.

Sermon: "Words We Cannot Say"
Judges 12:1–6

C. E. MCLAIN

The men of Ephraim prepared for battle; they crossed the Jordan River to Zaphon and said to Jephthah, "Why did you cross the border to fight the Ammonites without calling us to go with you? We'll burn the house down over your head!" But Jephthah told them, "My people and I had a serious quarrel with the Ammonites. I did call you, but you would not rescue me from them.When I saw that you were not going to, I risked my life and crossed the border to fight them, and the Lord gave me victory over them. So why are you coming up to fight me now?" Then Jepthah brought all the men of Gilead together, fought the men of Ephraim, and defeated them. (The Ephraimites had said, "You Gileadites in Ephraim and Manasseh, you are deserters from Ephraim!")

In this Old Testament story forty-two thousand Ephraimites died at the Jordan because they could not say a single word. The Ephraimites had come across the Jordan to battle the Gileadites, the people of God. But God strengthened the hands of his people, the Gileadites, and they put the Ephraimites to flight. In order to keep the Ephraimites from escaping, the Gileadites captured the places where the Jordan could be crossed. When any Ephraimite who was trying to escape would ask permission to cross, the men of Gilead would ask, "Are you an Ephraimite?" If he answered, "No," he was told to say, "Shibboleth." But he would say, "Sibboleth" because he could not pronounce the word correctly. Then they would grab him and kill him there at one of the Jordan River crossings. At that time forty-two thousand of the Ephraimites were killed.

Words are extremely important in human communications. Words in a given language change their meanings over time, so that what a word meant in one century may be completely different from what it means in a later time or place. But the meaning of some words never change. They may not be said as much in one era as they were said in another. When I came along as a child, I was taught to say certain words like "Thank you," "Yes ma'am," and "No sir." My parents taught my siblings and me that elementary manners and kindergarten respect will get a person in doors that a PhD can not knock down. When I read this Old Testament story of the Ephraimite threat made against the Gileadites, it is apparent that they lacked the ability or desire to say some important words. The Gileadites believed the Ephraimites were their ally. But when they called on the Ephraimites to help defend themselves against the Ammonites there was no response. The Gileadites were left to fend for themselves.

Let's look at this Old Testament Scripture, and let it give to us New Testament and contemporary meaning. What are the words that you have difficulty saying? Grade your own paper.

I. *Love* is a word many people cannot or refuse to say to certain people at certain times.

Many years ago an article appeared in the *Christian Century* magazine about a couple that had been married twenty-eight years. They were sitting before the pastor who had married them many years before. "Okay," the minister asked, "why are we here?" "He no longer says he loves me," the wife responded. Looking at the husband, the minister asked, "Sir, why don't you say that." The husband responded blandly, "When I married her I told her I loved her and if I ever changed my mind I would let her know." *Love* should be an easy word to say to anyone, especially those close to us. How sad it is when so many people need props, mood music, candlelight dinners, and special effects just to say, "I love you." We must not let Hallmark do all of our talking. The Ephraimites could not say the word *love*.

That is a shibboleth for many in our own country. During the height of the civil rights movement, Dr. King would move his troops to the hot spots of the South. When he got to Birmingham, the commissioner of public safety, Eugene "Bull" Connor, would gather his police department to confront King and the civil rights workers. Connor would confront the people seeking equal rights with police dogs, billy clubs, riot gear, tear gas, paddy wagons, fire trucks, loud cursing, and the machinery of city government. All King was going to talk about was love. The resurgence of the Ku Klux Klan, "neo-Nazis, skinheads, and other hate groups haven't learned to say "I love you" to ethnic groups unlike themselves. But not only does our nation suffer from the debilitating effects of racism; it suffers from the destructive pathology of self-hate on the part of many of its African American citizens.

The late Benjamin Harrison Roberts, when pastoring the First Shiloh Church in Houston, Texas, once said, "If you don't have enough love for everybody, you don't have any love at all." The spirit of the Ephraimites lives in many quarters. Many religions possess this Ephraimite tendency. The followers of many religions teach and practice hatred toward any group unlike themselves. Jesus says, "Those who say, 'I love God,' and hate their brothers or sisters, are liars; for those who do not love a brother or sister whom they have seen, cannot love God whom they have not seen" (1 John 4:20). In the Gospel of John (13:35) Jesus says, "'By this everyone will know that you are my disciples, if you have love for one another.'"

II. Other words difficult for people to say are "I was wrong."

The Ephraimites felt justified in their intent to destroy Jephthah and the Gileadites even though they chose not to respond to the cry for help from the people of God. There is no record of an expression of regret, an explanation for not responding, or any apology. There is only the threat and the effort to carry out the Ephraimite plot. Too often Christians neglect to help others or are bent on revenge and never repent. We are masters of excuses. The Scriptures teach, "Confess your faults to one another" (Jas. 5:16) There are countless instances in the Bible in which men and women would not or could not say, "I was wrong." In Genesis, when God came in the cool of the evening asking Adam, "Where are you?" Adam blamed Eve. When God asked Eve, "What have you done?" Eve blamed the serpent. When God asked, "Where is your brother?" Cain's reply was not, "I'm sorry; I was wrong" but "Am I my brother's keeper?"

In our National Baptist Church family there are now four national conventions. All stem from the same beginning. Could this be because someone refused to admit "I was wrong?" How many churches have split and a smaller weaker faction started because there was no effort to reconcile? How many homes have been torn apart because, whatever the source of the problem, neither the husband nor the wife refuses to admit "It was my fault"?

Jesus has admonished us to become reconciled one with the other, even when we bring our gift to the altar and remember that there is ought, a moral obligation, between us and our brother or sister.

III. *We* is another word that is difficult for many to say.

The Ephraimites could not think in the plural. They were the only people that mattered to them. They would not be inclusive. John Donne, the sixteenth-century poet, has written, "No man is an island; we are all a part of the main." We must be inclusive. No one is self-made. Everyone has been helped by others. We cannot eat or drink alone. We need so many others just to have breakfast. To have a cup of coffee we need others. We need the bean farmers from Columbia. We need the bean pickers, the inspectors, the packagers, the truckers, the inventory workers, the storekeepers, the stockmen and women, the cashiers and the bagboy.

We haven't added cream or sugar. To have cream we need the dairy farmers from Wisconsin. To have sugar we need the sugarcane farmers from Louisiana. To have hash browns we need the potato farmers from Idaho. To have bread we need the wheat farmers from Kansas.

We cannot be as the Ephraimites and not think inclusively. What if the Ephraimites had answered Jephthah's call? They would have helped defeat the Ammonites and shared in the spoils. But the Ephraimites would not stay close or stay with the

Gileadite people. There is a story told about a man who took his first boat ride with a friend out on a lake. Being a novice in the boat the man stood up in the boat. The wind shifted, and he fell overboard. When the man first came up to the surface, the man who owned the boat grabbed him by the hair, and his hair came off. The next time he surfaced the man reached out and took him by the arm, and his arm came loose. The next time the man surfaced the man grabbed him by his clothes, and his clothes began to tear. The man attempting to rescue the drowning man became frustrated. When he surfaced again the rescuer shouted to the man in the water, "Listen, I'm trying to save you. And if I'm going to save you, you'll have to stay together." Everybody needs somebody. In the cities of the plain, Lott needed Abraham. In Egypt Moses needed Aaron. Surviving Saul's attempts on his life, David needed Jonathan. To survive her first trip to Bethlehem, Ruth needed Naomi. When in prison, Paul needed Timothy. Even Jesus needed John the Baptist to be baptized.

IV. Too many people find it difficult, if not impossible, to say *God*.

The Ephraimites couldn't say *God*. They could only say, "We are coming over to burn your house down with you in the house." We should be able to say *God* because he is worthy of our praise and worship. When we are blessed with a good education, good health, a promotion, a good marriage, and good children we should say it is because of a loving God. There are consequences for failing to recognize him. Pharaoh couldn't say it, and his troops drowned in the Red Sea. When Ahab refused to recognize the God of Israel, Elijah announced there will be no rain or dew for three and a half years. There would be a famine in Israel. Nebuchadnezzar could not say *God*, and he ended up eating grass like an ox. Belshazzar could not say it, and the fingers of a man's hand appeared and wrote on the plaster of the wall during a celebration and pronounced his doom. When the New Testament opened, Herod refused to recognize the King of the Jews and he attempted to kill off all male babies in Bethlehem. He tried to find and destroy the new King.

When Jesus was brought to Pilate, Pilate washed his hands in indifference. Judas, one of the twelve, couldn't say it, and he hanged himself. Peter denied his Lord. In a moment of weakness even Peter, a close follower of Jesus, couldn't own his Lord. During the crucifixion two thieves hanged on their crosses with Christ. One couldn't say *God*, but God always has one who will call his name. One saw night, and the other saw light; one blessed him, and the other cursed him. One thief crawled into hell; the other climbed up into heaven. One wanted to come down, and the other wanted to go up. One was insulted; the other was inspired. In every situation, time, and circumstance, Christians of every race and nation should be able to say *God*. What is your shibboleth? What is that word you can not say? If we are to survive in this life and move on to the life to come, we must be able to say *love*, and "I was wrong." We must be able to say *we*, and we must say *God*. Amen.

6

How I Prepare to Preach

OTIS MOSS JR.

After reading Dr. Charles G. Adams's statement on how he prepares to preach in the first volume of *Power in the Pulpit*,[1] I am tempted to say, "My name is Otis Moss Jr., and I agree with this message, period." It is like asking one to give an A and B selection following a concert by Paul Robeson. However, I would like first to list a dozen-plus sources and resources out of which sermons have passed through my fallible earthen vessel for more than a half century. What I will list (with comments) is not a simple one, two, three process. It is not an A to Z Aristotelean syllogism in sermon preparation nor a Thomas Aquinas *Summa Theologica*, but rather a continuance of imperfect endeavors laid upon me by the "foolishness of preaching" (1 Cor. 1:21). Listed her are the origins of some of my sermons:

1. Experience with God and Holy Scripture expressed through texts that have used me for almost fifty-six years
2. Unceasing and fervent prayer
3. Meditation and miracles visible and invisible
4. Intense study and observation of all of life
5. Looking, listening, hearing, and learning from all experiences and all God's people
6. Loving people in the spirit of Jesus Christ with all my human frailties
7. Discipleship in Christ in joy, sorrow, and danger

8. Activism in great causes, causes worth living and dying for
9. Struggle and suffering
10. Remaining open to the Holy Spirit
11. Remaining open to the unexpected, the unpredictable, and sometime unwanted
12. Seeking an abiding communion with great ideas and the wisdom of the ages
13. Seeking to maintain a wholesome relationship with the past, present, and future

If one has a clear sense of the "why" of preaching, one can always seek to improve on the "how." Great technique devoid of anointment is like having improved means with unimproved ends. When I was a college student, while walking across the campus at Morehouse College, I heard a student yell from the dormitory window to a fellow student, "Hey man where are you going?" The friend answered, "Ah, nowhere, really." The young many in the dorm window said, "Wait a minute, I want to go with you." How often do our sermons have the above experience? Going nowhere and taking the congregation with us. In many instances it is perhaps less difficult to lead people nowhere than to take them on a serving, sacrificial, and prophetic journey.

Years ago in a ministers' seminar where Dr. Sandy F. Ray was the lecturer, we were given a charge and a challenge. Dr. Ray (the man Dr. Gardner Taylor called the President of Preaching[2]) said to us, "The preacher ought to have a gallery and a garden. You ought to have a gallery (a library) where you commune with the wisdom of the ages. You ought to know what great thinkers have said about certain issues and ideas. But you ought to have a garden where you can pull up plants from your own experience." You should be able to say with Isaiah, "I saw the Lord." You should be able to say with Paul, "I know in whom I have believed." You should be able to say with our ancestors, "I know I've been changed." Week after week as we journey through our "gallery" we ought to have now and then an encounter with Rudolph Otto's "Idea of the Holy."[3] There should be a meeting with what Tillich called "Ultimate Concern."[4] There should be some acquaintance with Martin Luther King Jr.'s midnight encounter with the divine, when he heard a quiet voice saying, "Stand up for righteousness, stand up for truth, God will be at your side forever."[5] This experience informed, enhanced, and influenced Dr. King's ministry for the rest of this life.

Several decades ago I heard an elder in the ministry describe a conversation he listened to between Dr. John Hope and a minister. My elder was not a participant in the conversation, just a privileged listener. Dr. John Hope was the first African American president of Morehouse College and the only college president involved in the founding of the NAACP. In the inspired conversation between Dr. Hope and this African American pastor, the pastor asked the esteemed college president, "Why don't you preach?" Dr. Hope responded, "I have not yet felt the urge to preach."

In his first letter to the church at Corinth, Paul writes, "Woe is me if I preach not the gospel" (1 Cor. 9:16). Sermons ought to arise out of a "Woe is me" urge, which gives us the "why" for preaching while the "how" is forever growing and maturing. Sermons ought to arise out of the urgency seen in the prophet's question "When God speaks who can but prophesy? (Amos 3:8). There must be a romance between one's calling and one's preaching. Harry Emerson Fosdick said of his preaching,

> Many times as I went to the pulpit I recalled Hugh Latimer's experience that Sunday morning when, headed toward the royal chapel, he heard a voice within him saying: "Latimer, Latimer, be careful what you preach today because you are going to preach before the King of England" then another voice said: "Latimer, Latimer, be careful what you preach today since you are going to preach before the King of Kings.[6]

Throughout our land there might be some who are trying to determine what to preach based on the desire to receive or retain a "faith-based grant." John the baptizer was not trapped in such trivialities. Jesus read the passage from Isaiah 61 and gave an eternal sermon shorter than the text and was almost lynched (see Luke 4:18–21; 29–30). Prophetic preaching can be dangerous. It is not safe but saving. Prophetic preaching can get you killed, but so can cigarettes, ribs, and pork chops. In my own preaching nothing is more basic than the unending affirmation that God is love. "Whoever does not love does not know God, for God is love" (1 John 4:8). Only love can bridge the gender, generational, racial, and ethnic gaps in our communities and nations. Love demands justice, and justice without love is brutality.

I believe great preaching is born of struggle and suffering. Therefore, the preacher must grapple with his or her own pain and the pains and profound hurts of the congregational members. There must be an open door between the pastor's heart and the hearts of the congregants. It is absolutely necessary to find time for silence, for reading, and for listening, as well as time for laughter, love, and romance with family. This requires mutual help and genuine support from family and congregation.

There are also moments when preachers must walk a lonesome valley where only God can journey with them. It is here that others must prayerfully and patiently wait with and for the prophet's return from the wilderness, the mountain, and the deep woods and forests of meditation and revelation. Since we live in a noisy and crowded world, we often think of retreat in the purely corporate or business sense—a time for strategic planning, marketing, branding, and bottom lines. We must forever relearn the meaning of being still. "Be still and know that I am God!" (Ps. 46:10) says the psalmist.

In the forced isolation of a jail cell came the "Letter from the Birmingham Jail."[7] It is a great expression of the blessed unexpected and unpredictable that can arise from an unwanted and painful circumstance. There are, however, some sermons that come forth from great hallelujah moments, beautiful moments of indescribable joy and gladness. Moments when we hear the angels singing. All of these and much more give birth to sermons and sermon preparation. "The word is near you," says Moses to the Israelites (Deut. 30:4,12–14). It is "'on your lips and in your heart,'" adds Paul (Rom, 10:8). The sermon is always a treasure in earthen vessels.

In preparation and delivery I use manuscripts, notes, and outlines. I begin with notes, focusing on a special Scripture and burning idea. Then I develop an outline using some of the notes. I then look at what others have said and written, seeking illustrations and examples. With all these things in hand, and uniting both head and heart, I try to write a manuscript. With notes, outline, and manuscript I prayerfully digest, agonize, alter, and sometimes rewrite until I have a path to open my heart to the congregation. And I'm always trusting God for some blessed experience and outcome. Inwardly, I take full responsibility for all the faults and failures, giving full glory to God for any blessing or benefit that flows from the effort. I seek to remember what Dr. Samuel Williams said to me and my classmates in seminary. The instruction was not original with him; it was passed on by Dr. Howard Thurman who received it from one of his professors: "No one is ever obligated to preach a great sermon, but everyone is eternally obligated to grapple with great ideas." I always add that if you spend a lifetime grappling with great ideas, somewhere in the course of your life you might, maybe, by the grace of

God, the love of Jesus Christ, and the communion of the Holy Spirit preach a few great sermons now and then.

Dr. Samuel D. Proctor followed the Hegelian dialectic—thesis, antithesis, and synthesis—with profound and everlasting impact. To hear a Gardner C. Taylor, a Benjamin E. Mays, a Mordecai Johnson, a Vernon Johns, a Sandy F. Ray, or Martin Luther King Jr. is to know without a doubt that God has sent some people into the world to proclaim the gospel. To hear a Dr. Renita Weems, a Bishop Vashti McKenzie, and the new prophets of the late twentieth and early twenty-first centuries is to know that God is still anointing women and men

"to bring good news to the poor.
. . . .
. . . to proclaim release to the captives
and recovery of sight to the blind,
to let the oppressed go free,
to proclaim the year of the Lord's favor."
(Luke 4:18–19)

One essential aspect of growth in preaching is to keep one's eyes, ears, mind, and heart open to the past, present, and future. I am continually blessed in my conversations with my son, Rev. Otis Moss III, and his generation of young men and women whom God has chosen to be the voice and vision of the new century. God is still moving, speaking, acting, and liberating. Jesus is alive forever and ever.

Sermon: "Ministering to a Murderer and All God's Children"
Acts 9:10–19

OTIS MOSS JR.

If our ministry is to follow the ministry of Jesus, we must minister to all human beings and become stewards of all creation—God's creation. We like to be selective about the persons to whom we should minister. Too often we recoil from ministering to murderers because we believe it is easier to murder murderers than minister to murderers. We have designed hangman's nooses, electric chairs, lethal injections, gas chambers, firing squads, and all forms of killing as a substitute for ministry. We have designed a language to absolve ourselves of guilt. There are certain types of murder we call *homicide*, which is to be punished in certain instances by another murdering process called *execution*. Homicide is to be condemned and punished while execution is to be applauded and rewarded with all the instruments of government. This is true especially if the condemned murderer is poor and identified as a minority.

Some might quickly point out that we do not all have the same ministry gifts. Therefore, some are not gifted for the same ministry. This indeed is true and is the powerful and compelling reason why we need family, village, and community. Every true community is ecumenical. Every real family is blessed with diversity. We should not take statistics, physics, music, and physical education out of the curriculum because some professors

94

cannot teach them. I cannot teach computer science, but I am amazingly blessed by those who can and will. We need an inclusive ministry. Can you imagine what might have happened to all of us if someone had not been called to minister to each of us?

Rabbi Abraham Joshua Heschel, a leader, scholar, teacher, and writer, one who marched with Dr. Martin Luther King Jr., declared, "Few are guilty, all are responsible."[8] Jesus said, "'I have come to call not the righteous but sinners to repentance'" (Luke 5:32). If we cannot minister to murderers and all sinners, we have no reason for ministry. If we cannot minister to all God's children, our ministry becomes an exclusive, selfish, and elitist enterprise designed for certain people and not all people. Jethro ministered to a murderer named Moses (Exod. 2:18–25; 3:1). Nathan ministered to a murderer named David (2 Sam. 12:7–14). Ananias ministered to a murderer named Saul, also known as Paul, an apostle of Jesus Christ.

Let me share two moving historic experiences, one from Texas and one from South Africa. The first experience was told to me by Rev. Jesse Jackson Sr. during his presidential campaign in 1988. While campaigning in Texas, Rev. Jackson talked about his experience in Selma, Alabama, in 1965, one of the history-bearing, world-changing moments in the modern civil rights movement. After the speech a white gentleman came up to Jesse and stated, "I was at the Selma March." Before he could complete his statement, Jesse said, "Wasn't that a great moment?" The white man said, "You don't understand; I was there with the Ku Klux Klan." Then he looked at Rev. Jackson as tears welled in his eyes and asked, "Will you allow me to take a photograph with you? This time I want to be on the right side. I would like to share this photo with my grandchildren. I want them to know; this time I was on the right side." The photo was taken. They shook hands and departed on higher ground.[9]

If Jesse Jackson's campaign had done nothing more than minister to an ex-Klansman, the effort would have been exceptionally worthwhile. It did so much more, but time, space, and words are not adequate to tell the whole story. Barack Obama is not just running for president of the United States of America; he is ministering to a nation that has since 1619 (and before) been murdering dreams, hopes, and the bodies and the souls of men, women, and children—Native Americans, African Americans, Hispanics, the poor, women, and others who have been despised, denied, rejected, scorned, marginalized, massacred, lynched, raped, persecuted, poisoned, and left on the stony and bloody road of the valley of the shadow of death.

The second experience was witnessed by Rev. Dr. Joan Brown Campbell in South Africa. One night before the elections in 1994, Rev. Campbell and others noticed the Honorable Kenneth Kaunda and a white South African shaking hands and embracing. The white man was seeking forgiveness from Mr. Kaunda because he had been given the assignment by the South African Security Forces to murder this great man. That night he asked forgiveness. It was granted.[10] Bishop Desmond Tutu is right: "No Future without Forgiveness"[11] This is the appropriate title to one of Bishop Tutu's inspiring books. It is literal fact and truth for family, church, and nation.

Cardinal Bernardin made a special trip while cancer was invading his body to minister to a young man who had sought to destroy the cardinal's career as a priest by a false accusation. The accusation was made in a highly explosive atmosphere and caused much suffering to a man literally dying of cancer. The cardinal chose ministry over murder.[12]

For a little over twelve years, Dr. Martin Luther King Jr. was minister and prophet to murderers and the children of the murdered. Rabbi Abraham Joshua Heschel said, "Martin Luther King, Jr. is a voice, a vision and a way. I call upon every Jew to harken to his voice, share his vision, to follow his way. The whole future of America will depend on the impact and influence of Dr. King."[13] Few people realize that one aspect of Dr. King's work was redirecting the energies and destinies of gangs in Chicago. Many people do not realize that Mrs. Coretta Scott King brought gang leaders to the Martin Luther King Jr. Center for Nonviolent Social Change in the early 1990s to introduce them to the power of nonviolence as the most creative instrument for social change. One of the gang leaders asked Mrs. King if she would be his "surrogate mother."

Our nation has national jails for gangs but no national ministry for gangs and gang leaders. There is, however, a new generation of men and women in ministry with a sense of mission and ministry to our sons and daughters who are caught up in this violent interplay of mutual self-destruction. They are committed to the ministry of a "more excellent way." One day in the ancient city of Damascus, God spoke to a disciple of Jesus named Ananias and directed him to minister to a murderer named Saul of Tarsus. Ananias, in "realistic" human expression, says in substance, "This man is a murderer; I and all my friends are on his 'hit list'." He is an enemy to Jesus and all his followers. Lord, do you know who this murderous fanatic is? He breathes threats and murder against your disciples." In my own words (inspired, I pray) the Lord responds to Ananias: "Ananias, you know Saul's past. I know his future. I knew him before you knew of him. You are fearful of his yesterdays; I have reequipped him for all his tomorrows. Today I give you a ministry assignment. Do not call him murderer; call him brother. Be his friend, prayer partner, and faith partner."

Ananias is instructed to do three things:

1. Lay hands on Saul
2. Baptize him
3. Give him some food

What a ministry! A ministry to the fallen, failing, fractured, and feeble. A ministry to the weak and the wicked. A ministry to the pathetic and the petty. A ministry to the weird and the wounded. A ministry to the ugly and the unjust.

1. Pray with them.
2. Lay hands on them.
3. Baptize them.
4. Feed them.

In some strange and dangerous ways we are all guilty. "Whoever does not love does not know God, for God is love" (1 John 4:8). "Whoever does not love abides in death" (1 John 3:15). Whoever does not forgive is a murderer.

When we feed our children unhealthy and unholy diets we are murderers.

When we deny our children healthcare, daycare, safe homes, safe streets, and excellent and safe schools, we are murderers.

When we refuse to end poverty, war, and racism, we are murderers.

When we practice sexism, immigrant bashing, and zenophobia, we are murderers.

When we refuse to stop the spread of HIV/AIDS locally, nationally, and internationally, we are murderers.

When we refuse to care for the infected and give them the best in care, and search diligently for a cure, we are murderers.

When we leave 47,000,000 Americans in the cold without healthcare, we are murderers.

We must therefore pray with one another, lay hands on one another, and offer baptism to one another. We must feed one another food for the mind, body, and spirit. If we refuse to do these things we are murderers. We need a ministry for murderers and all sinners, for all have sinned. We must forever minister to one another. We must minister to the failing and the promising.

When we minister to one another, we discover a Moses hidden in exile.

When we minister to Moses, we discover a Joshua.

When we minister to one another, we nurture a Samuel.

When we minister to the exiled, we embrace a Ruth and we welcome a Mary, mother of Jesus.

When we minister to all of God's children we raise up a Coretta Scott King; we welcome a Fannie Lou Hamer.

When we minister to one another, we claim a Denzel Washington, whose acting is in Hollywood but whose anchor is in West Angeles Church of God in Christ.

When we minister to one another, we march with King, Tutu, and Mandela.

When we minister to one another, we claim a Joseph and reclaim a David.

When we minister to one another, we claim an apostle John and redeem a Paul.

When we minister to one another, we discover saints and redeem sinners.

7

Preaching the Prophetic Contradiction

OTIS MOSS III

Rap Artists like Talib Kweli have been raising a primary question for preachers and of preaching by asking, For whom and to whom are we speaking? In his song "Where Do We Go?" Kweli points to the glory of a generation that is both as valuable as a pearl and as discarded as a broken shell. How are we to speak to a generation of great power and potential who are exiles of the church and live in modern-day, tragic contradictions? Dr. Walter Brueggemann, Old Testament professor emeritus of Columbia Theological Seminary, created the term "exilic preaching" to describe this postmodern, homiletic moment of destiny and despair, fused together by the social forces of racism and marketplace mentalities.

The conversation of preaching has changed and transformed since we arrived at this postmodern, exile moment. No longer can we assume that this exilic community understands our language, our stories, and our spirited style of presentation. The preaching community is accustomed to *native* worshipers who understand the unwritten codes of black religious engagement. The *natives,* as theologian Leonard Sweet has titled them, understand the call to worship, the hymns, the praise, the call and response, and the rhythms and the rhetorical tradition of black church. We love preaching to this bunch. They truly *get* the intimacy and intricacies of the black church experience. The nuances mean something to them. But what of those exiles who have no reference point for black worship? Their understanding is filtered; they view the church through the lens of the media, hip-hop culture, and street rhetoric. From their perspective, the church and specifically the preacher are seen as irrelevant at best. The televangelist, on the other hand, who often ascribes to the nonprophetic preaching tradition of prosperity, receives the highest level of visibility in our culture. Those preachers currently rule the airwaves and have an unyielding grip on the microphone. And people are listening.

The popularity of prosperity preaching is rooted in the nonthreatening, status quo doctrine it promotes. And it is a doctrine easily embraced by the conservative, evangelical culture that never challenges structures of race, class, or gender and does not speak truth to power. Those preachers have significantly veered from Jesus' commission and directive to set the captives free and to preach good news to the poor. So to be an effective, postmodern interpreter, it must be integrated into the preachers' subconscious and become an integral part of his or her daily theological practice.

The unique, cultural call of today's preacher is that we are called to preach within this prophetic contradiction. So what does it mean to preach prophetically and to preach in contradiction? It means simply this: the proclaimer of the Word must raise the pressing issues of race, class, and gender while infusing them with human tragedy and frailty. This exilic generation wants to hear about the contradiction of humanity while also hearing about the grace of God. Within the black religious tradition, it is called preaching with two voices. Historically, those within the black preaching tradition have been able to *speak* with a blues sensibility and celebrate with good news eschatology. The timeless writings of James Baldwin, Toni Morrison, and Langston Hughes; the poetry of Sonia Sanchez and Paul Beatty and the music of jazz legend John Coltrane; as well as the work of contemporary artists Dead Prez and Common, speak to the contradiction of the human condition and human suffering.

Tragedy and triumph, joy and pain, all wrapped in the same spirit, are at the heart of the black religious tradition. It is important to understand human failings and fragility when one preaches about God's grace. Our worst moments can define us, but they also inform our personal testimonies. The brokenness of the characters in Toni Morrison's *Beloved* illustrate that fact; and even the tragedy of John Coltrane's drug use and the long-term foolishness of black Baptist sexism, when mixed with the prophetic call of the collective community, can enable us to grow tall enough to wear the crown of spiritual integrity in the face of human frailty.

Prosperity preaching unfortunately truncates the gospel into a formula of abundance and monetary blessings, turning Jesus into a cosmic bellhop or a drive-thru bank machine. Prosperity preaching is congruent with the values of market-driven hip-hop. The ethos of gangster rap artist 50 Cent is identical to the ethos of the prosperity evangelists. They share the same material goals and value individual security and lifestyle above community and individual sacrifice. The prophetic model dares to question conventional wisdom with the values of hope, faith, justice, and love. When the preacher is in tune with the stories of the *thug and the theologian*, a new homiletic is created where the preacher is able to reach exiles and lead them into a meaningful dialogue with native worshipers.

So how is that dialogue created? When one is engaging in postmodern, prophetic preaching, prayer and the proper reading of the biblical text is primary. Message formation should begin with a thorough reading of Scripture—not from the vantage point of a preacher but from that of a reader and a believer. The preacher in most of us has a tendency to seek out a sermon while believers and readers allow the Word to sit, simmer, and twist in the imagination so they can raise the *right* questions about the nature of God. The practice of reading the Bible with no agenda is difficult for most preachers, for the Sunday morning sermon looms large in our consciousness. But we must make every effort to read the Bible not as proclaimers but as those who believe deeply in the text's truth. When we release ourselves from the obligation of being authorities, we hear the Word with different ears. While I attempt to read the Bible in this manner, I often shift into preaching mode because the press of Sunday is heavy on my spirit. But when I am able to release myself and read the Word for personal development, my imagination and God's inspiration take me places I would not have seen as a preacher.

I keep a daily journal of my thoughts, prayers, goals, and spiritual insights. When reading the Bible I raise questions about the text. How does the Word speak to the reader? What is the cultural context? What empire—Roman, Assyrian, Babylonian, or Egyptian—is the current colonizer? I record these insights along with other ideas, quotes, thematic material, poems, and novels that relate to the text. For example, I have found that Franz Fanon is very helpful for understanding the book of Daniel. Reading Fanon taught me how colonized people view the world, like Daniel who is told he must give up his name. August Wilson's work is insightful for reading the Psalms. His writing is about the poetry of language lament and reclamation. Zora Neal Hurston's prose can breathe new life into the Exodus narrative. Just reread *Moses, Man of the Mountain.*

I use my journal as a guide and a tool, as I translate biblical stories into modern language. For example, the narrative of Jesus on the cross states he was "hung between two thieves" (John 19:18). My translation has a theological twist. I say that he was hanging between two "thugs." This gives a modern entrance to an ancient text and allows me to create a framework of understanding for and appealing to the "unchurched" ear. A thug on the cross has different theological implications than that of thieves. Thuggish behavior has become a common, cultural norm for exiles. The translated text is now speaking to both the hip-hop and bebop generation. The hip-hop generation connects with the thug motif and the bebop generation—native worshipers—are familiar with the story and mentally agile enough to accept prophetic imagination with fresh ears.

After laying the groundwork through prayer, study, meditation, and journaling, I create an outline defining what I see in the text and how it relates to the relevant question. Does God's love extend to thugs? Or why does God use thugs to do divine work? These questions are at the core and contradiction of the human condition. What do thugs—Peter, Moses, and David—bring to the table of faith? To get the answer, I am forced to think with a dual consciousness. Exiles hear the Bible as outsiders and are listening for ways to allow this world to enter their lives. So I must engage the text as an outsider while reading it as an insider in order to ensure my reach. Music and films that raise profound existential and theological questions are extremely popular with this unchurched generation. The movies of Tyler Perry and Matrix Films, as well as the music of Common and Talib Kweli have found a special place in the exilic culture. With the spiritual yearning of exiles, prophetic preaching combined with existential exploration is needed to speak to the total personality.

The outline is created and the message is sharpened and focused, so now I can create a manuscript. As I write, I move easily between urban-inspired hip-hop and the musical, improvisational language of bebop traditions. I may begin with a poetic flow rooted in the formality of the sixties and seventies and then shift into the open *break it down* illustrations and language of the postmodern culture. I am speaking to more than one generation, and I recognize that my calling and my gift is the ability to serve as a homiletic bridge builder and interpreter. To borrow a phrase from my friend Rev. Tony Lee, "I want to rock it from the streets to the academy."

Since my current church, Trinity United Church of Christ in Chicago, is multigenerational and both native and exile, I have a special obligation to be sensitive to the multiple stories and testimonies within the congregation. The sermons I preach must be contemporary and traditional, academic and street, hip-hop and bebop, prophetic and pentecostal. That is the role of the prophetic interpreter. One must speak to human frailty and proclaim prophetic power, and it is the calling and responsibility of my generation to speak the prophetic contradiction.

Sermon: "When Thugs Get Saved"
Judges 11:1–11

OTIS MOSS III

The way you start is no indication of how your journey will conclude. And starting from behind does not mean that your destiny is inextricably bound to the back of the pack. That's a proven athletic fact; ask any coach who has experience in the area of track and field. The greatest long-distance runners come from the continent of Africa, specifically Kenya. "Kip" Keino, the famed long-distance runner and coach, instituted what we now call "high-altitude training." Coach Kip, as he is affectionately called, discovered that the rigors of training at higher elevations prepare the body to adjust and deal with lower altitudes.

Coach Kip trains all his runners to spend time at higher elevations. Anyone who enjoys track and field or the Olympics will notice something different about the Kenyan style of running. When Kenyans run, they always run in a pack. They want to make sure everyone on their team comes in first, second, or third. Also, you will notice that Kenyan athletes never start by leading the pack. As a matter of fact, they spend the majority of the race bringing up the rear. If you watch the Olympics, you will assume the Kenyans are going to lose. If it is a 30-minute race, and you watch 24 minutes and 59 seconds, you will be convinced that the Kenyans will come in last place.

But something happens toward the end of the race. It's at this precise moment that the Kenyan runners begin to kick and expend enormous effort. And when they kick, they utilize those muscles that were trained at high altitude and low oxygen in an effort to handle the low-altitude and high-oxygen conclusion. Because Kenyan runners have been trained at a high altitude with low oxygen, it is easy for them to run past the competition during a low-altitude, high-oxygen moment. When Kenyans kick, they alter their physical positions and their thought processes, which ultimately changes their conclusion. At first glace, it might appear that Kenyan runners, who started from behind, might remain behind. But their starting lineup, their initial positioning, doesn't mean that the finish line is not within their grasp. How they start out is not how they end up!

So it's not how you start in life's race that is important; it's how you prepare, and it's how you finish and conclude. Just because you started out one way doesn't mean you have to remain in that particular state. Change your position, and that will change your conclusion. Most of us believe our sociological condition is the same as our spiritual destiny. The collective and socioeconomic factors that shape the physical condition and psychological reality in our community do not have final word on our destiny. If your destiny is to do great social justice works for God, your family, your friends, and your coworkers, then ultra-conservative public policies have nothing to do with your destiny. The problem is, we are constantly tuned into and dialed into the wrong frequency forecasting our conclusion.

Technology has truly enhanced my daily life and my ministry. I love my iPod. I listen to music on my iPod. I listen to sermons on my iPod, and I regularly download social and political podcasts. But I *always* download the weather report. When I am not in Chicago, I make sure to download the weather report because the Windy City is incredibly unpredictable. On one particular occasion, when returning to the city, I downloaded the weather podcast for Chicago. I listened to the report, which stated it was going to be warm and sunny. Warm and sunny, that worked for me. That was good. So, I prepared for warm and sunny because I'd listened to the downloaded podcast. I was ready and properly equipped to go back home. But when I arrived in Chicago, it was cold *and* cloudy. I was mad and fussed at my state-of-the-art technology because I thought the weather reporter had messed up. But I had messed up. I downloaded a different day and the wrong report. I was listening to a past report that had nothing to do with my present reality! Are you getting this thing?

That is exactly what the enemy does. The enemy wants you to listen to your past reports that have nothing to do with your present reality. Just like the Kenyan runners, how they start out running is not how they finish the race. So delete whatever the devil downloaded into the computer chip of your brain. Your past is just the prologue and not the final chapter of your journey. If you are willing to understand that God has greater things for you, then God can transform your life.

According to our text, Jephthah was a mighty warrior who was the son of a prostitute. His father was Gilead, and his mother was a prostitute. Eugene Peterson's biblical translation states that he was "the son of a whore but he was a tough warrior." His father Gilead stepped outside of the boundaries of marriage and slept with another woman. And if one looked at this text with a hermeneutic of suspicion from a womanist vantage point, one might say that Jephthah's mother was probably not a prostitute but just a woman who was caught in a web of sexual power relations. In order to protect a man's integrity within a patriarchal society, a man would often label the other woman a prostitute, especially if he had forced himself on her. He could keep a degree of integrity by violating her integrity. But that is another sermon, so I will leave that alone for today.

So back to the text where the Bible says Jephthah was a mighty warrior and the son of a prostitute. He was a mighty warrior *and* the son of a prostitute. You missed it. He was a mighty warrior, *but* the son of a prostitute. Are you getting this thing? Your dysfunction has nothing to do with your destiny. You can start out one way, but you don't have to end up that way; that is not your conclusion. God will use the marginalized, disenfranchised, dismissed, disregarded, distressed, demonized, outcast, and oppressed for the kingdom's good. Jephthah was a mighty warrior, and the son of a prostitute. To the people we say God cannot use, God says, "Come here. I can use you." The Bible records Jephthah's dysfunction but also gives account of his destiny. And some of us are afraid to deal with our dysfunction. We only want to engage our destiny. But I'm here to tell you, you don't need to clean your slant or sanitize your history. God can deal with your past. God can deal with your problems. God can handle your imperfections. The kind of God we serve can deal with your dysfunction *and* take you to your destiny. This is the beauty of what is called the "scandal of grace," according to German theologian and martyr Dietrich Bonhoeffer—God loves the people we do not love.

Scandal of grace—we all can relate. If people only knew the dungeon you crawled out of to make your way to church this morning. If people only knew the kind of mess in your life, the kind of dysfunction in your family, the kind of hell you go through. If they knew the kind of pain behind your shout and behind your song, it would make somebody's head spin. But thanks be to God you're still here! I don't know if anybody here has ever been through anything and you're just glad you made it into the house of the Lord this morning, but you are here by the grace of God! Upload into your spirit that your dysfunction cannot stop your destiny. Dysfunction may change your testimony, but it will not stop your destiny.

When we look at the text, Jephthah is in conflict with his family. He is like most of us, a product of dysfunction. Jephthah's brothers run him out of town with the help of his stepmother. I cannot imagine the pain placed upon one's spirit when those who are supposed to love you push you to the margins of society. In a perfect world, Jephthah's family would support him, but sometimes blood will block your blessing. Sometimes the very people charged with caring for you are also the ones trying to destroy you. Jephthah's brothers spoke against him, but his father was silent. He is not unlike many of young brothers caught in the prison industrial complex who are clueless about the name and whereabouts of the one they call father. We know Jephthah's lineage, but his daddy says nothing. How many of our children who have been kissed by nature's sun live a life of exile because Daddy was silent,? Jephthah's daddy was silent and as a result of the father's muteness, he was now a child living in exile in the land of Tob. Here we find something interesting in the text. We have all the historical, cultural, rhetorical criticism necessary to help us understand the intended narrative and metaphorical meaning of the text. But absent is the powerful, transforming agent called love.

Jephthah's family had an issue with his lineage and refused to love a boy born in a dysfunctional situation. Without love our children live in exile. You can talk about lineage, heritage, and culture, but if you don't have love, this tragic oversight will crush the fragile hearts of children. And that lack of love leads to "thug life." When love is removed from the equation, we are left with empty children craving the very thing they have not received. Our society, even the church, does not like the word *love*. We like other words. We like *blessing* and *anointing* and *going to the next level, hallelujah!* We like to hear about *increase* and *sowing seeds*. We love to talk about *God hooking us up*. Love must come back home to take residence in our theological vocabulary. What the world needs now is love; the gospel is clear. Love is a spiritual discipline. God is Love! Love has power. The missing element for this generation's development is an understanding of divine love and self-love freed from the limitations of market-driven, nihilistic indulgences. One might call it *old school love. Old school love is*

the kind of love that is rooted in community and commitment.

This kind of love says, "Take your hat off when you come inside."

This kind of love says, "No sir and yes ma'am"

This kind of love says, "Pull your pants up boy! Stop showing the crack of your behind."

This kind of love says, "Don't curse in front of your elders!"

This kind of love made us hold our heads high in the face of oppression.

This kind of loves tells us, as poet William Cowper did in "Negro's Complaint," "Fleecy locks and black complexion cannot forfeit nature's claim; skins may differ, but affection dwells in white and black the same." This kind of love says, "You don't have the right to get a D in school. You don't have a right to get an F. Do you know who died for you?" I am talking about that kind of love. The kind of love that says, "Dressing like a pimp isn't cute, and dressing like a stripper *ain't* sexy!" It's the kind of love Grandma demonstrated when you messed up your Easter speech, yet she still put her arm around you and said, "It's alright baby."

When you have love in your life you walk different, you talk different. You act different when somebody loves you. It is the long-time peace activist and minister William Sloane Coffin who said, "It is not because we have value that we are loved, but because we are loved that we have value." French philosopher Rene Descartes was wrong when he said *Cogito ergo sum;* "I think therefore I am." But as Coffin observed, it is *Amo ergo sum*; "I love therefore I am." And if we are to reclaim our children who have been written off, we must begin with love. Love has power. Love tells a broken person, "You have oil wells pumping in your living room." The power of God's love is as simple as waking up in the morning. There is something profound in the African American tradition when a witness of God's glory shouts, "The Lord woke me up this morning!" It is the theological narrative speaking from our ancestral tradition. It is not just God who woke us up. It is the theological motif wrapped in this simple folk statement. God's grace casts a loving shadow on a people economically exploited, politically abandoned, and theologically demonized by Western culture; yet God's concern is not redacted by race, class, or gender.

God loves us enough to wake us up to fight another day. "I am not done in your life," says God. "You still have things to do." And I stopped by to say to you this Sunday that "God is not done with you!" You still have speeches to write, books to author, businesses to start, sermons to preach, letters to read, children to inspire, poems to perform, food to cook, cures to create, boys to raise, children to love, hurdles to jump, rivers to cross, and mountains to climb. How dare you hang your head! We are children of the most high God.

So Jephthah had no love in his life. They sent him to the land of Tob. He was an exile in the land of Tob. The word *Tob* means "good place." I'm coming back to that in a minute. Because love did not live in Jephthah's house, he was put on the path to thug life. Remember, Jephthah was hated because of his lineage. His brothers hated his heritage. His father was Gilead, but his mother was a prostitute. The brothers hated him because of his DNA. The brothers feared his heritage because when Jephthah became a man he would be in position to upset the economic structure. His connection to his father meant he was in position to receive an inheritance. Jephthah's brothers had to disenfranchise him in order to protect the economic order. Inclusion of Jephthah in the boardroom meant a new redistribution of family wealth. And the brothers weren't sharing.

We recognize Jephthah's pain because we have experienced the hatred of our heritage. Our fleecy locks and dark complexion points to our roots on the continent of Africa. The institution of slave codes, the Dred Scott Decision, Plessey vs. Ferguson were all attempts to drive us into the land of Tob. It was not just color or lineage but fear of losing power or having to share wealth with another member of the family. The text states that the brothers did not want to share their inheritance with Jephthah. The brothers instituted their own segregation policy to protect their financial resources. Racism is not solely rooted in color but is a socially constructed demonization of black culture, designed to keep people of African descent disempowered and separated from the institutions of social-economic empowerment.

Jephthah was living the thug life in Tob. The Bible states that he lived with outlaws. In the OM3 translation—for the uninitiated that is the Otis Moss III translation—Jephthah lived with thugs. The Hebrew meaning of *Tob* is "a good place." It does not make sense for the place of excommunication and exile to be called good. But sometimes a setback is a setup for God to do something in your life. Even though his family did not want him, there were thugs who said, "We will embrace you." There were thugs who said, "We will love you and we will train you." God will provide a new family if your old one rejects you.

Let me break it down so you understand what I am attempting to say. I believe it was Pastor Howard-John Wesley of St. John's Congregational in Springfield, Massachusetts, who introduced me to this illustration. When you go into some of the new public restrooms there is an interesting setup. After you do what you came to do, the only way to get rid of the stuff in the urinal is to turn and walk away. You cannot flush it away. You have to turn away from the mess so the sensor knows you are done with this chapter of your journey. If you keep facing the mess, it will continue to linger, but if you turn and walk away it will be permanently removed. The only way to get rid of some people in your life is to turn and walk away and let God do the flushing.

So Jephthah is living the thug life in Tob. But this is a good place, because God is preparing to use his thug skills for a kingdom blessing. Let's talk about thugs for a minute. There are several things I like about thugs. Thugs are loyal. When a thug is down for your cause, you do not have to worry about a thug skipping town or calling in sick on the day of your protest. Sometimes, I would rather have a thug behind me than some church folk, because I don't have to worry about the thug stabbing me in the back! We serve a God who has a special place in God's heart for thugs and thugettes!

God rolls with a brother named Peter. And anytime Peter gets in trouble, he pulls out his switchblade ready to cut somebody. When Jesus died, he hung out with two thugs on a cross. When God picked his greatest apostle, he called for a thug from Tarsus named Saul. Jesus loves thugs. So, yes, thugs are loyal. And thugs tell the truth. If thugs don't like something they tell you. Ask a thug on the street, "Why don't you come to church?" The thug will give you an honest answer: "There are hypocrites up in there, and I know I'm a hypocrite, and I know I'm not doing right." See, you know church folk will try to act perfect and will sanitize their lives, not realizing we all have a little thug history. We have thugs in our family. We have thugs as our friends. Now, here is the good news: thugs can reach other thugs. There are some people we will never reach, but all it takes is *one* thug to tell somebody the truth about the transformative, saving power of Jesus.

When a thug gets saved, he is able to communicate with many that most saved folks want to dismiss. Jephthah is now living in the land of Tob. Living the thug life with his crew. But watch what happens now. This thug is on the outskirts and doesn't think he'll ever come back home. Then all of a sudden the same people who kicked him out say, "Come on here. We need your thug skills to destroy the Ammonites." And Jephthah says, "Hold on, hold on, hold on. Ain't y'all the same folk who kicked me out? Ya'll rolled up on me deep and said you ain't getting none of this. So then I found a crew in Tob that surrounded me with love and now you want me to come back?"

Jephthah wants to know why he is now being sought. They want him back because he has expertise in insurgency. They want him back because he has expertise in guerilla warfare, and they don't know how to deal with the Ammonites because their policy was ill-conceived when they engaged them in war. Those in the land of Tob realized they needed somebody with a thug mentality who can handle that thing. And so Jephthah makes the decision to go back. But on one condition: he will go back if he is in charge. "I'll roll back up in there if I'm commander," Jephthah says. They said, "Let the Lord be a witness between us. If you defeat the armies of the Ammonites then you will be in charge."

Oh, my goodness! Oh, my goodness! This thing gets me so excited because I like how God orchestrates the situation. Because we serve a second-chance God—oh, I'm sorry, a third-chance God. No, no, 4th, 5th, 6th, 7th, 8th, 9th, 10th, 11th, 12th, 13th, let me know when I get to your house. Fourteen to 19; did I get to your house yet? Twenty to 38; did I get to your house yet? Thirty-nine, 40, 41–43; am I there yet? We serve a God who will give you another chance. Is there anybody here? Has God ever given you a second to fifth chance? Then go ahead and praise him like you've lost your mind. God will give you another chance. But here's the thing: Jephthah is thankful for his haters in the land of Tob. He is grateful for their lack of insight. You completely missed it. Contemporary and popular comedian Kat Williams says, "You've got to be thankful for your haters. If you've got one hater, you need about five more. If you've got five haters, you need ten more. Haters do what haters do. Haters just hate." If you are doing God's work, you are going to have haters. So come on, haters, hate on me. It just means you are going to elevate me and take me to another level. Is there anybody here who has haters in your life? You thank God for your haters because your hater taught you how to pray. Thank God for your haters.

I've got to give this personal testimony. I've got to share this story. There are people who will try to write you off and send you to the land of Tob. But we serve a God who will give you a second chance. When I was in high school, a counselor told me I did not have the intellectual capacity to go to college. He called and told my parents that they ought to think about finding a technical school for me because the standardized tests indicated I did not have the intellectual capacity for higher education. Well, let me tell you how God works. Several years ago,

I was in Shaker Square in Shaker Heights, Ohio. I was eating all by myself, not bothering a soul. I was just eating my lunch at Pierre's restaurant in Shaker Square not bothering anyone.

I looked up from my meal and realized the high school guidance counselor who had told me years before that I wouldn't amount to anything and would never be successful was serving me my lunch. "Do you remember me?" I asked. "You said I wouldn't go to college, but I've been to Morehouse College, and I've been to Yale University, and I'm now working on my PhD." Look what the Lord can do! Look at God. What God's done for me, God will do for you! God will! Sometimes you've got to give God praise for your haters. And God will save thugs because God loves thugs. God calls the rejected. God calls the broken. God calls thugs. God calls thuggettes. God calls those living on the margins. I'm not talking to the "bougie" folk. I'm talking to the folk who've got a little thug in them.

Do I have any thugs in the house today? Holla back if you hear me! I want you to know that God can save you. If God can save a drunk like Noah and use a pimp like Abraham, a hustler like Jacob, a thugette like Deborah, a baller like Sampson, a player like David, a player like Solomon, a ghetto soldier like Peter, and a roughneck like Paul, God can use you. God can use me. God can use us. God can save thugs. Is there anybody here? Do you know God will save thugs? God will save families. Say yes! Say yes! Yes, God will. God will. Yes, God will! God will save a thug. God will save you. Do I have a thug in the house? You don't know why you came here today, but you came here for this moment. God wants you to be a part of God's kingdom building, and it's your time right now to make a commitment to God. When thugs get saved! Things are about to get easier for you. When thugs get saved. God is about to bless your life. There is a thug in here tonight. Your Mama dragged you to church, but right now you are the one who is going to be an apostle in thug life. God wants you to make a decision. The doors of the church are open right now!

8

Preaching from the Overflow

RAQUEL A. ST. CLAIR

As I have tried to make conscious and intentional that which I do almost automatically in preparing a sermon, I have noticed a change of perspective that has ineradicably changed my sermon preparation. I believe that this fundamental shift in orientation has infused my preaching with new power and taken it to another level. When I began preaching, I thought of preaching as an event, an act, a moment. It was something that took place at a certain time and in a certain place. And while this is indeed true, this "blocking out" of the preaching moment into this discrete moment of time caused me to miss the myriad of connections between preaching and other aspects of my life. To be sure, preaching was always connected to my intentionality in seeking to live out in my daily life the gospel that I proclaim. What it was not connected to was my care of self, the greatest resource, second only to the Good News, that God had given me.

During this season of intermittent nagging from the Holy Spirit and my seeking God to understand what God was getting at, I sensed that God was challenging me to invert my view of preaching and its preparation. I knew that God could use broken and broke-down people in amazing ways—God was using me! Yet what I felt God pushing me to do was to live in such a way that I could preach primarily out of the overflow rather than from the emptiness. The realization that there were many ways in which I was not caring for myself while trying to care for others occurred after my father's death. I was grief stricken and about

115

thirty pounds overweight. I used food to help me handle the final stages of his cancer. Actually, I had used food to handle all stressful situations. My father's death did to me what death does to many. It forced me to consider my own mortality: how I wanted to live and what legacy I wanted to leave behind. I began a process of self-examination, perhaps better described as life examination. I began to look at myself spiritually, physically, socially/emotionally, and financially to see how I cared for and considered these parts of myself. I reflected on whether these parts of me were full or empty, what strengthened and what depleted these areas, and what I could do to change what I did not like and what I had to leave in God's hands to work out. My list was longer than God's.

As I began the process of self-evaluation and improvement under God's management, I began to notice how strengthening these areas of my life was strengthening my preaching. Indeed, God was calling for a prepared Word, but God was also calling for a prepared preacher—someone who in the process of taking care of God's vineyards had not forgotten to take care of her own (Song 1:6b). Therefore, my preaching preparation began with preparing myself spiritually, physically, socially/emotionally, and financially, and then preparing the Word out of the overflow that comes from tending my vineyard. So in the pages to follow, I would like to humbly share my sermon preparation process, which is becoming more of a lifestyle and less of an event. I do not present this as something that I have mastered but as a journey that I have undertaken and continue to pursue.

The preparation of the preacher can be summarized in one word: discipline. To discipline a person or a group means to put them in a state of good order so that they function in the way intended. Discipline, in spite of a popular misconception, is not inherently stern or harsh. Bible translators chose *disciple* as an appropriate term for one who learns by following.[1] Discipline, used in this way, is not about punishment but training. It is the instilling of certain practices and behaviors that help one to accomplish certain goals, achieve a particular end, or fulfill one's purpose. I believe that effective preaching and effective living both require discipline.

SPIRITUAL DISCIPLINE

My best sermon ideas have been birthed out of regular, consistent, daily Bible reading. My Bibles are a diary of my walk with God through the Word. Around November or December, I choose a Bible and read through it during the year. I find a Bible with a one-year plan that allows me to read from a single book or letter each day so that I can maintain the narrative flow of what I am reading. As I read, I underline the verses, phrases, and/or words that speak to me. In the margins, I write my questions, comments, or one-line prayers and mark each with a date.

I do a combination of formational and informational reading. I read formationally, for my own spiritual development, to hear how God wants to address me through the Word. While I read, I ask God three questions: (1) "What is my Word?" (2) "What are you saying to me or my particular situation?" and (3) "How do I apply this message to my daily living?" Sometimes my attention focuses on a particular verse that I commit to memory and then see its application at a future time. At other times, I receive the insight I need, the answer to a question, or some strength to deal with a particular issue. More often than not, I am simply refreshed from my time of listening and reflecting on the Word.

Formational reading enables me to be in a place where God can deal *with* me *about* me. It is my therapy of sorts, allowing me a safe space in which to gauge where I am, what I need, and what I need to do. Formational reading puts me in the "pew" as God speaks to me through the Word. It is my act of consistently reminding myself that there is a Word from the Lord *for me*. Formational reading instills a level of humility, reminding me that I am not exempt from being proclaimed to; that it is not the people who need a Word from the Lord but I who need the message. It allows me to receive *my* Word—to hear it, feed on it, reflect on it, and ultimately embrace it. In this way, I am fed before I feed others. None of us walk away from the preaching experience empty because a disciplined devotional life that includes the reading of Scripture means my sermons are birthed from the overflow of the Word. Because I have spent time in the Word for me, I do not give my meals away. There may be morsels to share but not at the expense of the preacher.

Informational reading, on the other hand, centers on content. It focuses on the who, what, when, where, why, and how. The goal is to remain familiar with the subject matter of the Bible. I tend to read chapters from a particular book or letter during a single sitting, ultimately finishing it. I read to follow the flow of the passages and to become familiar with the author's style and use of language. In this way, I can pick up on key terms or phrases. I can hear when certain themes are repeated and begin exploring them. I notice the repetition of names or places or actions. I pay attention to phrases, themes, or motifs in one book so that I can recognize them should they appear in another. For example, there are interesting parallels between the mariners' experience on a boat with Jonah and the disciples' experience on a boat with Jesus. I can then compare them to see if the authors are doing the same thing or building on past images in a new way. These parallels and differences become grist for my sermon mill.

When reading informationally, I seek to hear the author on his/her own terms rather than blend the various witnesses of Scripture together. There's a reason that we have sixty-six canonical books instead of one. They are not saying the same things the same way. There are nuances and subtleties that can be heard if one will listen. When I read Mark's Gospel and then turn to Luke's, I notice the differences in the telling of the same story. Exploring these differences allows me to see some things I might have missed by merging these stories together in my mind without hearing the witness of each evangelist. I begin to question why one added a detail or another left it out. I examine the placement of the passages to see if the same material comes before and after the passage or if the authors insert it in different places of their narratives. If the placement is different in each Gospel, I ask why and how does it affect the interpretation?

As I read the Bible formationally and informationally, I remain open to sermon ideas. I listen for passages that will preach. I jot down these Scripture references in a preaching journal. If I have any insight or direction about the development of the sermon, I include it. If I already can see the points or have an illustration in mind to illumine the text, I write it down. Sometimes, there is only the Scripture and a question pointing in some direction for future exegetical exploration. I use this preaching journal in two ways. First, my preaching journal is my memory book. It is critical as such because my personal devotional time and sermon-writing time are two separate and distinct occasions. I use it to recapture points I would have forgotten if I had not written them down when I first had the idea. I have learned that I have to retain ideas on paper until I have a chance to work them through, or else I will lose them. If a sermon idea, insight, or point comes during my devotional time, I scribble down as much as of it as I get during that initial spark and return later to flesh it out fully. I also note whether I think this sermon idea is enough for one sermon or can be expanded into a sermon series.

My preaching journal is also my reservoir. All preachers have dry spells. When the revelation and inspiration for preaching seem hard to find, I flip through the pages of this journal to see if anything catches my attention, and I then begin to develop it. I may go back to an idea I had months or years ago and realize that now is the time to preach that word. I have learned two important preaching lessons from doing this. The first is that sometimes I have had to experience some things before I could preach ideas I had previously gotten. Second, sometimes I have had to get to the other side of certain situations, seasons, or trials before I could preach some texts or sermon points I had written. My preaching journal and the daily Bible reading from which it springs prevent my dry spells from forcing me to preach a Word before it or I am ready.

Prayer is another essential component of spiritual discipline. I keep a prayer journal. My journal is predominantly dedicated to me. It is where I enter into conversation with God by laying bare my thoughts, feelings, wishes, and desires. My journal is not a place of traditional or formal prayer but rather an open conversation where I invite God into my time of personal reflection on the day that has passed and prepare for the day ahead. My journal is the place where I can be truly honest with God and bring myself into God's presence without pretense. It is an uncensored work where I am not trying to say the right things but tell it like it is, at least from my perspective. I just *am* when I journal, and from there I allow God to do whatever or say whatever God wishes to me.

My prayer journal is a record of my journey. It provides tangible evidence of prayers prayed and prayers answered. It helps me to discern the voice of God because it allows me to keep track of what I heard or thought I heard and judge if I heard right. Most important, my journal is an essential preaching tool because it provides a safe place for me to be naked and vulnerable so that I can be appropriately transparent in public. It provides a place for me to house my frustrations and disappointments without spewing them from the pulpit on people who have their own issues. Ultimately, my journal is a place for me to uncover my wounds, mourn my losses, examine my pain, and invite God in to heal me so that God can staunch the blood before I "bleed" on others.

Daily worship is another aspect of spiritual discipline that aids in sermon preparation. By worship, I simply mean taking the time to adore, honor, and reverence God for Who God is. During my personal worship time, I take the time to turn my petitions of "will you" into the praise of a "thank you." Worship keeps me grounded. It reminds me that I am not the center of anything, including the preaching endeavor. When we are overwhelmed and overworked and underappreciated, it is easy to think that we are doing people and God a favor by being faithful to the call on our lives. Worship not only reminds me that there is a

Someone greater than me that I can depend on but that preaching the gospel is a privilege.

PHYSICAL DISCIPLINE

I used to take better care of my truck than I did myself. I was careful what kind of gas I used (what I fed it). I took it in for regular mainte-nance. Meanwhile, I was living off of fast food and takeout and rescheduling doctor's appointments because I was too busy (that's code for too big). With a family history of heart disease, diabetes, high blood pressure, and various forms of cancer, my doctor wanted me to lose weight. She wasn't mean or cruel about it. She just stated the facts and let me know that I could greatly reduce my chances of developing these conditions by simply dropping a few pounds. I hadn't done that and wasn't working that hard to do it. After all, I told myself, in the grand scheme of things, I am not that big. But my spirit was troubled.

One day the Lord made it very clear to me. I was sitting in my office having just completed the sermon found in this book. I said to the Lord, "This sermon is asking people to step into whatever you told them to do. What do you want me to step into?" As clear as day the image of my treadmill appeared in my mind's eye. I sensed that the Lord was telling me that I would literally have to "walk into my [next] season." I began to exercise sporadically at best. A personal trainer from our congregation came to me, not knowing my struggle, and offered his services because "the Lord laid it on his heart." I delayed a little while longer.

Then the connection came. I realized that I was preaching before I even opened my mouth. From the moment I entered the pulpit, I was saying something about my relationship with God through the care (or lack of care) of my body, which is God's temple. I began to ask myself, "What am I saying with my physical appearance?" and "Is it getting in the way of what I am preaching?" My goal was and is not to achieve some societal ideal of beauty but to honor the body God gave me and keep it in working order for as long as possible. Moreover, I continually pray for the power to preach God's Word. Yet I had to ask myself, "Can you handle the power?" In other words, if God were to honor that prayer and grant me the power I desired, could I *physically* withstand it? Consequently, I began a program that included both cardio and weight training. I needed my body to preach. I needed physical stamina to say it like I felt it. Therefore, physical discipline in the form of exercising, eating better, and getting proper rest became an act of sermon preparation because they cannot hear without a preacher (Rom. 10:14) and the preacher cannot preach outside of her body.

SOCIAL/EMOTIONAL DISCIPLINE

It was odd for me to begin thinking about my personal relationships in terms of a discipline. However, I began to recognize that discipline, "putting [my relationships] in a state of good order so that they function in the way intended,"[2] was necessary. Like many preachers, my life was dominated by the ministry. Everything and everyone else were secondary. My planner told the story. Preaching engagements were highlighted with a yellow marker that could not be erased. Everything else was written in pencil. Opportunities to fellowship with family and friends were usually the first items cut when ministry required more of my time.

I knew things had to change, and one experience in particular drove that message home. I had returned home from the church a little earlier than usual. As I was driving up to my garage, I noticed that the motion sensor on the garage had not triggered the light to come on. When I got out of my truck, I walked in front of it to see if my motion would be detected and the light would come on. I saw the small red light flashing, letting me know it had registered my motion, but there was still no garage light. I began walking into the house, complaining about another thing I had to fix. Then it hit me: the light was not coming on because it was still too bright outside to trigger it! I was so used to coming home after dark that I did not realize that the light was not supposed to come on. I stood there in my driveway trying to figure out when was the last time I had both left for work and returned from work in the daylight. I could not remember it.

In that moment, I knew that I was going to have to be intentional about developing and maintaining my personal relationships and not losing myself in ministry. I set a goal of at least one social, non-church-related activity each week. It might be dinner with friends, a night at the movies, a play date with my nieces, or a family gathering. However, I either had to go somewhere other than church and my house or spend time in my home with someone who does not live there. These times of fellowship are now given at a minimum the same level of importance as any church meeting, event, or counseling session. I therefore use the same standard for cancelling with my family and friends as I do with cancelling a ministry activity. During these dedicated blocks of time, fellowship is my ministry.

Making time to be in relation with others grounds my preaching in the concrete experiences of life well lived. My interactions with others become fodder for future sermons. I receive great sermon illustrations and firsthand anecdotal material, and I encounter real-life questions that ask if there is any word from the Lord. In short, talking with and sharing life with others gives me something to think about and pray about that may turn into something to preach about. Of course, I never share without permission, and I guard others' privacy as I would my own. However, being in the company of others outside of the church allows me to hear how people really feel and think instead of how they feel they are *supposed* to think. Simply listening and spending time with others allows me to preach in ways that are relevant. Spiritual discipline feeds my soul. Physical discipline feeds my body. Through social/emotional discipline, I nurture myself through relationship building. This is what feeds my heart.

FINANCIAL DISCIPLINE

My financial stewardship begins with the tithe and includes Spirit-led giving. I pray about what God would have me to give above and beyond my tithes whenever an offering is received. Financial discipline built on the practice of giving tithes and offerings reminds me that God is the provider and owner of all I have and that I am only a steward entrusted to honor God with my resources. Honoring God with my finances means giving my tithes and offerings, paying my bills on time, living within my means, and saving for the future. By consistently doing these things, I avoid becoming stressed out about money. Financial discipline not only relieves certain financial stresses but purifies my motives in preaching. It prevents me from becoming a "hireling" who preaches for the money rather than one who preaches because of the ministry. Although I do believe a laborer is worthy of her hire (1 Tim. 5:17–18), money should never be the determining factor in ministering the gospel. I am often asked if I preach in "small churches." My response is that I preach where I am invited and where God leads. No gathering of believers is too small. Nor does the preparation change. I prepare and preach to two as I would two thousand.

Financial discipline also helps me to avoid preaching to please people. Although I want people to enjoy the preaching moment and to feel that it was worth their time to listen, I do not feel obligated to "shout" at a congregation so that they give more money when the word God sent me with is one of introspection or sacrifice or repentance. Since my sufficiency lies with God, I can be true to the message I have been given and strive to preach to God's satisfaction. God will supply what I need and open the doors of opportunity. When we are financially disciplined, our own houses are financially solvent. We can then free ourselves of the temptation to preach for the money. Instead, we can engage in spiritual, social/emotional, and physical discipline because we can take the time to refresh our spirits, relate to those around us, and rest. This is the overflow from which God has called me to preach.

Sermon: "Wet Feet"
Joshua 3:1–13

RAQUEL A. ST. CLAIR

I need to ask y'all a question, and it's a question I wouldn't dare ask some people because they are so *holy* that they may not get my struggle. So I figure I'd ask y'all because maybe you can understand where I am coming from. Now, I know what the Bible says about my situation. I know that the psalmist says,

> Wait for the LORD;
>   be strong, and let your heart take courage;
> wait for the LORD!
>
> (Ps. 27:14)

I know that Job says,

> All the days of my service would I wait,
> until my release should come.
>
> (Job 14:14)

I know that Isaiah says,

> Those who wait for the LORD shall renew their strength,
>   they shall mount up with wings like eagles,
> they shall run and not be weary,
>   they shall walk and not faint.
>
> (Isa. 40:31)

And I know that Paul says, "Do not grow weary in doing what is right, for we will reap at harvest time, if we do not give up" (Gal. 6:9). But I have to ask you, have you ever been weary of waiting? Have you ever had what God said not match what you see? Have you ever had your rhema (right now word) not match your reality? Have you ever received a prophecy that did not match your particular circumstance? Maybe it's just me. But sometimes, I get weary of waiting.

Some of us are weary of being in Egypt. We are weary of serving hard time, making bricks without straw, and having Pharaoh boss us around. Others of us are waylaid in the wilderness. We are blocked, not bound. We are blocked because although we are free in the wilderness, we can't seem to get to the fullness of the promised land. Like the children of Israel, we too have our Red Seas and Jordans to cross. And whereas there are many similarities between the crossing of the Red Sea and the Jordan in that both are bodies of water, both were the boundaries into new territory and a new season, both were encountered and crossed by a command of God, and both required God to make a way for God's people. There is one key difference. At the Red Sea, the waters will not part until God moves. But at the Jordan, the waters will not part until we move. At the Red Sea, we have to wait. But at the Jordan, we have to wet our feet.

Both situations require the same miracle—water to give way to dry land. But in each instance, God uses a different method. And I think that we sometimes get stuck and then weary of waiting because we want God to do in the wilderness what God did in Egypt. We want God to do again what God did before just like God did it before. So since God sent a little windfall to pay the bill last time, we are staring at the mailbox instead of putting 10 percent in the tithing box this time. Since God answered the prayers of the saints on our behalf last time, we've been calling the prayer warriors instead of calling on the Lord for ourselves this time. We fail to realize that what God did in Egypt was to get us to trust God at the Red Sea. And what God did at the Red Sea was to get us to follow God through the wilderness. And what God did in the wilderness is to get us ready to fight for the promised land. At each stage of the journey, God is making us take more and more responsibility for our journey.

Along the way, we may need some of the same miracles as before. We may need another way made, problem solved, bill paid, or our bodies healed. We may need another mountain moved, burden lifted, door opened, or prayer answered. The last time God did it without us. But this time, God may only do it *with* us. The Red Sea will part while you wait on the banks. But in our text for this morning, the Jordan only parts for wet feet. So if you are weary of waiting, standing on the banks of a river you cannot cross alone, and no east wind has come to part the waters, maybe you ain't at the Red Sea. Maybe you're at the Jordan, and you cannot cross the Jordan like you crossed the Red Sea. You see, the Red Sea was pure grace in action. God took the Israelites as they were—whining, complaining, faithless, and rebellious. For four hundred years, they had cried to the Lord for deliverance, and God sent Moses to deliver them. Yet at the first sign of trouble, they tell Moses and God it would have been better if they'd stayed slaves.

But at the Jordan, the people had to sanctify themselves before they moved. They prepared themselves physically, spiritually, and mentally to do what God said. When we sanctify ourselves, we are just getting ourselves in position to say "Yes" to the Lord. We are making up in our hearts and minds to say "Yes" to the stuff we know God is saying and getting ready to say "Yes" to stuff God hasn't even said yet. Notice the difference in the Israelites. At the Red Sea they whined, but at the Jordan they walked. At the Red Sea, they complained, but at the Jordan they consecrated themselves. At the Red Sea, they were faithless, but at the Jordan they followed. At the Red Sea, they rebelled, but at the Jordan, they believed and followed their leader. And here is why their reactions are critical: slaves can live in the wilderness but they cannot enter the promised land.

Some mess is only tolerated in slave quarters and in the wilderness when we didn't know any better or hadn't grown enough to do any better. However, that same mess is unacceptable in the promised land because we have seen better, know better, and therefore should act better. There is enough grace at the banks of the Red Sea for even the rebellious to cross. However, that same mess will not cut it at the Jordan. At the Jordan nobody said a contrary word about where they were going, or what God was doing, or the one God chose to do the leading.

They just did what they were supposed to do, beginning with those in authority. At the Jordan, leaders have to go first. Then people have to submit to God's appointed authority not because they have no other choice or the enemy is pressing hard behind them, but because they choose to follow.

In our text, Joshua commanded the priests to carry the ark in front of the people. The water would not recede until their feet got wet. Then they had to stand in the middle of the Jordan until the others crossed over on dry land. They remained until twelve stones were placed to commemorate the place where their feet stood. Finally, they crossed over and resumed their position in front of the people. We have to act according to the position we expect to have in the promised land while we are still in the wilderness. If we feel called to have position in the promised land, we must step up to the plate on this side of the Jordan. If we are to lead in the promised land, we must follow spiritual authority in the wilderness. If we are called to minister in the promised land, we must serve on this side of the Jordan. If we are called to preach in the promised land, we must prepare on this side of the Jordan. If we cannot get in line with God at the banks of the Jordan, then we are not ready for the promised land. In other words, we have to become promised-land people before we can be promised-land possessors. We cannot live in old ways and expect God to do new things.

So after the Israelites consecrated themselves, they had to follow behind the ark of the covenant. They had to follow the presence of God and go where God went because the children of Israel had not been this way before. In similar fashion, we can only cross the Jordan at the time, space, and place that God leads us. We have to follow God's leading and movements in our lives. And the good news about following God is that if we follow, we will never be any place where God isn't already. Because when we follow God, God will be our guide and go with us. God will be our compass and keep us company. God will be our map and march with us. Yet at the Jordan, we are often tempted to stay in the wilderness because the only thing that compels us to move is the word of the Lord and our frustration with the wilderness. Unlike the banks of the Red Sea, there is no Pharaoh or army threatening from behind. At the Red Sea, we had to cross or be killed. We had to cross or be slaves. However, the wilderness can be a place of slow death. It kills you softly. You can stay there a good 40 years or more and even eat manna while you stay.

That's why some of us are stuck right now. We've been in the wilderness so long that we've begun to forget about the promised land. Instead we've developed a wilderness welfare mentality. As long as we get our daily supply of manna, an occasional quail, and shoes and clothes don't wear out, we won't move. We can become so dependent on what God is giving out that we are no longer attentive to where God is going nor responding to what God is commanding. If we are not careful, the ark will have crossed over and the waters will have closed up and we will be left behind because the only way out of the wilderness and across the Jordan is behind the ark following the Lord. And be prepared, because the Jordans of our lives require another level of faith. We are going to need more than Red Sea faith to cross the Jordan. At the Red Sea, a tithe seemed sufficient even though Malachi 3:8 says we have robbed God in tithes *and* offerings. But at the Jordan, a tithe will only keep the locusts away; you will need to add an offering for the overflow. At the Red Sea, coming to church only on Sunday mornings was OK. But at the Jordan, you have to actually get involved in ministry; give, not just get. At the Red Sea, reading and praying on the fly got us through. But at the Jordan, it seems like we have to prioritize time with God before God prioritizes time with us. At the Red Sea, we could grumble, mumble, and complain. But at the Jordan, those Red Sea attitudes could keep us out of the promised land.

The Jordan requires another level of faith because at the banks of the Jordan we run the risk of being embarrassed, at best, and drowned, at worst. At the Red Sea, you can wait for dry land before you move. But the Jordan requires wet feet. God requires us to walk in the water before any dry land appears. The Jordans of our lives require our participation. They don't just happen. They will happen, but only if we move. At the Jordan, God will tell us to get prequalified for a mortgage and look for the house before God shows us the money for the down payment. God will make us apply to school and get into school before God will show us how we can schedule in school or pay for school.

The Jordans of our lives require a greater level of faith and our participation because at the Jordan, God flips the script. The

Lord tells Joshua not just to cross the river but to cross it during the flood season when the Jordan has overflowed its banks. When we stand in the banks of our Jordans, the Lord will tell us to move, to cross over at a time when we are the least likely to make it on our own. In other words, God tells us to commit to something that we know, God knows, and others know we cannot finish by ourselves. At the Jordan, we need God to move, yet God makes us move first.

Is that where some of us are right now? In a place where God is asking us to do what is impossible, undoable, or incompletable by us? Is God telling you to tithe or go beyond the tithe, and you can't see how to pay your bills? To start your business now instead of when you think you will be better prepared? To answer your call now instead of continuing to put God on hold? To buy that house or look for a house now even though you think you should rent a little longer? To take that new job when you are tempted to stay where you are because you've gotten used to the manna and quail in your wilderness? And let me tell you, there's nothing inherently wrong with the wilderness. Sometimes God sends us there like God sent Jesus. God will feed us there like God did Elijah. God will give us water there like God did Hagar. The problem with the wilderness is staying there after your lease is up. One may have to rent some space in the wilderness, but we were never supposed to buy property there. So I need to tell somebody who is standing on the banks of the Jordan that the movement of our feet becomes the catalyst for the movement of God's hands. Wet feet trigger working hands.

So when will God push back the waters, you ask? It may be when you push off your sandals and get in the water. Like the priests, you may have to step off the banks, feel the chilly Jordan on your legs, and squish some mud between your toes. You may have to feel a fish or two brush past your ankles. You may even have to stand there a little while before the waters recede. But don't be afraid. Even though you are standing in the Jordan, you are still standing, and God's about to move. And so my task is simple. I just need to tell somebody, whoever you are, to consider this: Perhaps the key to your breakthrough is wet feet. Perhaps you are waiting on God, and God is waiting on you. Perhaps it is time to step in what God told you. Because according to the book of Joshua, you only get the territory you step in, not the stuff you name and claim from far off. For the Lord has said, "'Every place that the sole of your foot will tread upon, I have given to you'" (Josh. 1:3). In other words, you cannot secure it until you step on it. The bottom line is that we cannot get there unless we get up and go. We cannot take it unless we take a step. We cannot possess it unless we proceed. We cannot conquer until we cross over. We will not win until we wet our feet!

9

The Power of Narrative Preaching

WALTER S. THOMAS SR.

For the past thirty-five years I have spent my life preaching the gospel and sharing the good news of Jesus Christ. I must admit I never thought this would be the plan or path of my life, but, I must confess, I have no regrets. I thank God for giving me the privilege of telling the redemption story and, in the words of Phillips Brooks, sharing that truth through my personality. I grew up in the emerging era of television and in the era when we still went to the library. I remember the *Lone Ranger, Zorro, Leave It to Beaver, Wagon Train,* and *Bonanza* television series. In either a half hour or hour, we watched plots form and resolve themselves as we sat glued to the twelve-inch, black-and-white screen. On weekdays, we would go to the library and check books and novels around such varied topics as baseball biographies, science fiction, and historical events. Getting a library card was a rite of passage. Now that I am grown, going to the movies serves the same purpose, and I will rush to the movies on opening day of a great film.

My upbringing gave me a fascination for stories and storytelling. I remember being consumed by the books I read and staying up late into the night to finish the story and see how things would end. I think this experience also helps define the way I see life and the world. I believe that we are living a story and that the dramas we see on television and in movies is but a snippet of the drama we live every day. I see the story line in everything we do and in everything that happens. These foundational understandings are critical to understanding sermon formation and preaching styles. This age is even more video conscious than those of us who are first-generation television. There are video iPods, PSPs, PlaySta-tions, Xboxs, Nintendos, DVD players, YouTube, and a host of other platforms for visual presentations. The eye and the mind are being drawn to the stories that are now told everywhere. Persons stroll the large book stores and sit and read and feel the power of stories breaking all around them. The café is more than a place for coffee and a bun; it is the place to relax and spend a moment reading and then reflecting.

We are a people of stories. We know our African American heritage from the storytellers of our childhood. I have vivid memories of my grandmother reciting the poetry of Paul Lawrence Dunbar and Langston Hughes. I remember the elders of the family telling us the stories of our family. They spoke of the early days of our family and the relatives who were in our lineage. These stories were passed on from generation to generation. The griots of our history have told us the story of our history in this land. We have seen our history in their ver-bal presentation, and we understand the truth that was left out of the textbooks.

Having been born four years before Brown vs. Board of Education of Topeka, Kansas, I was well acquainted with a system that promoted separate but equal. We lived with an uneasy tension, and that tension has found a new home in preaching. When we saw blacks confront racism by marching into the streets of America, we knew that new doors were opening. I remember watching the young men and women integrate Ole Miss, and on national television I watched Jack Ruby shoot Lee Harvey Oswald. We lived with questions, and in most instances the answers were not acceptable. Why racism? Why so much pain? Why limited opportunities? Why couldn't we go into certain stores as we traveled south? The answers to these questions caused new questions to be raised. I do not still live in that world; indeed, things have changed. Yet I am still forced to question the situations that life dares us to face. Now, however, I seek to find the answers from my stance as a Christian and not just as a fellow participant or actor in the drama of life.

Over the years I have forged a particular style of preaching, and, to be honest, it is still a work in progress. The need to address the human situation, to be existential, however, has always been the cornerstone. I read Scripture, and I see the story line and the situation that is being presented. Even if am reading the letters of Paul or the General Epistles, I see the story, the history, the moment when the person uttered these words. In my mind, Scripture is not only given for inspiration; it is also given in a context. There is an original situation that gives birth to the utterance, and that situation is pregnant with truth and meaning. When we quote Jesus saying, "Not my will but thine be done" (Luke 22:42), we must understand that the context "Gethsemane" is God's continual revelation to his people. My aim is to help persons find the meaning of God in their lives and to help them come to grips with the scripts of character development that God is writing for them. My aim is not just to answer the question of what is God going to do about my situation, but also to help persons understand and appreciate God just for who God is.

For me, the Scriptures are the launch pad into the situations that persons are facing. They serve as the passport into the peculiar places where people live. When I read the Scriptures, I see both the past and the present. I see the condition in its original moment, and I see how it has morphed to today. I see my task as that of helping persons see God in what they are facing. I really do believe that God is developing us through the situations that we face and that we are called to develop. We must face our challenges and grow. We must stand in our circumstances and become. We must deal with our pain and struggle and "come out like gold" (Job 23:10). Life is not intended to defeat us, though at times defeat seems eminent; God has purposed us to overcome.

Central to my hermeneutic is the *reality of the resurrection*. There is no doubt in my mind that the resurrection is one of the most powerful revelations given us by God. He raised Jesus from the dead. It is a historical event. It happened on the morning of the first day of the week. Yet it happened within a particular context. The followers of Jesus were disheartened and ready to give up. They were afraid and defeated. The work that Jesus began was about to end with him when suddenly he rose! His resurrection was the revelation that we can never count God out. The ancestors of our faith put it this way: "He may not come when you want him, but he's always right on time!" His resurrection proved that even when there appears to be no reason to hope, God can and will still move. This truth guides my preaching and my living. If we believe that God raised Jesus from the dead, then we can believe that all things are indeed possible. God is always hanging around the edges of the text, waiting to make God's presence known. The resurrection tells us that God is never finished until God says so. God is actively waiting and working to accomplish God's plan. History is just that: *His Story!* My understanding of preaching and ministry are intricately tied to this belief: *God raised Jesus from the dead,* and God will raise us when life signals our defeat.

In this regard, I am strongly influenced by *liberation theology.* My training at Howard University's School of Divinity in the mid-seventies helped me to see the value of this theological point of view. In Christ God was liberating a community from the oppression of every force and every oppressor. He was setting them free to be free. For me liberation theology celebrates the presence, the *is*ness, and the wonder of God while affirming God's help and support in our quest to become. We cannot make it without the help of God. I am an existentialist in that I believe that we must find the meaning in our lives, but I do not see God as just there to "fix" our issues. God is to be known and embraced for who God is. God's qualities and characteristics are as important as my search for meaning.

In fact, my discovery of meaning is also my discovery of God. As an African American, liberation theology, which identifies the oppressed as the focus for God's activity, enables me to expand the definition of oppression to include any force or factor that limits our ability to become fully whole and fully free. I read the sacred text with this kind of liberation intent: God is setting us free. My question then becomes: Free from what? What idea? What force? What impediment? Are we free to become whatever it is that resembles our higher self? One thing is for sure: freedom is the issue. Sin has left us in and with bondage. We are constrained in the very world in which we were created to conquer. This is our lost opportunity. This is our repressed dream. This is the distant memory that our preaching is called to revive. We are reestablishing the family of God and helping persons find their way home and find their way to real freedom. Every time I rise to preach, I am guided by these thoughts and seek to fire a bullet of liberating truth and not buckshot of sermonic rhetoric.

Preaching is a noble art and science. It is *art* in how we present it; it is *science* in the message we present. My style is what I choose to call *narrative preaching.* It is not just telling the story that grips me. It is the nuances of the drama and the tensions within the story that guide my preparation. I see myself as a movie director, determining where to focus the camera and how it should be presented. In the model that I use, there are three distinct elements to the narrative. They are the *character(s),* the *setting (context),* and the *incident (situation presented).* Without these three there is no story. Moreover, the sermon is found in the tension between any two or all three of the factors. In this regard, I am indebted to Dr. Samuel D. Proctor for his use of the dialectic in preaching. The sermon, the meaning of life, the discovery of truth, the revelation of God are found in the tensions of the factors. My task is to expose *a tension,* as the text may have several tensions. The sermon is more than just a summary of the facts or an exposition of each verse. It must be taken as a whole and presented with all of its strange twists and turns. My task is to sit in the director's chair and help persons identify with the characters, the settings, and the situations in such a way that they embrace the transformation that is taking place before their eyes. There is always a tension, and preachers must decide where it is and how to reveal it. Our exegesis gives us insight into the workings of the story, and the Holy Spirit gives us direction in how to present it.

In planning to preach from a specific passage, I spend time identifying the three elements and looking carefully at the "script." For me the text is the screenplay. It is the written drama that needs to be presented. It is a story about freedom and about individuals understanding the meaning of God in their lives. It is the basic story that begs to be told. When I decide on a text and identify the three elements, I look for the tension that exists between any two and then focus my lens on that tension. I want to see how it affects the characters. I want see how it affects their thinking and their actions. I want to see my situations and myself in the script. This is what I call *the point of identification.* It is at this place that the sermon becomes not only appropriate to be preached but essential. It is now needed information. Before I look at word studies or exegetical material, I take my seat as the director of the movie. I look at where I will focus and what it is I want others to see. I am aware that each director reading a script will tell a different story by the places where the emphasis is put. I try to make the story seem real in the present. Dr. Evans Crawford, professor of preaching at Howard said, "Any sermon that starts in the Bible, stays in the Bible, and ends in the Bible is not a sermon." I want the sermon to come to the present and to be alive in the here and now. I spend a large amount of time trying to decide how to present the story and the truth I have found.

My next step is to conduct research both on the text and on the truth or tension I am dealing with. I use a wide range of materials, including novels, movies, Google searches, anecdotes, nonfictional material, and even family experiences. They are then woven into the story to give it further clarity. Clarity is critical, and relevance is essential. As the director of this drama, I have the license to explore the depths of the character, the setting, or the incident and to make the connection with what is happening in our times. I am presenting *a life situation,* and I am telling the story through the life of someone who lived centuries ago. Yet the key to the story is always God. He is not merely the Lone Ranger riding into town; God is always present, and the situations of life teach us that truth. With every sermon and new understanding of human beings, I always try to make God's case and to help the people understand the God who saves. Yet I feel compelled in each sermon to explore the frustration that is inherent in our human position. The call of God is always a call to revisit self and to embrace God. This is a key principle that I try not to violate. The sermon however, cannot conclude without *celebration.* God has stepped in and has made the crooked way straight. The celebration comes because now we understand; now we can do; now we are free; now we have power. The new understanding has set us free. His Holy Spirit has broken the bonds of oppression.

I think word studies serve the preacher well in trying to present the text. The nuances of a tense or mood of a verb can open up a text to major insight. I believe every passage in the Bible can preach; we just have to find the story in the text. Now, I think every preacher must have a command of the history of the Old Testament and the New Testament. The history is the story, and we must be more than familiar with the story. We must know it well. I research archeology, politics of the period, social arrangements, and any other material that will help me tell this story and present this truth. I start with a tension that reveals a truth. I then try to show how that truth is worked out and worked throughout the text. It is a truth revealed by God and a truth that is discovered by humans.

My mission when mounting the desk is to make sure this movie is good. Dr. D. E. King, late pastor of Monument Baptist Church in Chicago, told me to "always be open to revelation." In other words, let God speak while you are speaking. I write my sermons out in their totality, but I preach them aware that God might change parts of them and/or expand others, that the movie may have to show in parts (if it is too long!), or that the audience may get the truth without hearing it resolved in the sermon. When I finish preaching, I am quick to write in the margins any new revelation I received.

The key to any great novel is the plot. The same is true for the sermon. There must be a plot. For me the plot is born out of the creative tensions in the text, but it must be presented with all the skill and craftsmanship that the preacher can muster. The story must be told in such a way that the hearers cannot totally anticipate the next move. There must be *unanticipated suspense.* The story must take some twists and turns; the truths must be deep below the surface of the text; and listeners must have an "aha" moment. I firmly believe that there are always deep truths and awesome revelation to be mined deep below the surface of the text. I read the passage over and over, trying to break new ground with each reading. I interact with each character at a variety of levels, trying to discover the truth that may not have been seen but gives new insight on the text and its truth. I then tell the story that has the new truth at its core. I must admit, I do enjoy telling the story, painting the picture, building the movie, and bringing it to conclusion. Jesus Christ entered our narrative and forever changed it. He opened new doors of understanding and presented the kingdom of God with such power that to be allowed to help persons glimpse him and come to know him is the challenge that stirs me every time I sit with the script known as The Bible.

Illustrative material must be chosen very carefully. Some stories that are stories in their own right when improperly woven into the sermon can do great harm to the focus being put forth. I have biblical stories that are good for illustrations. I seek to parallel the story I am telling with some other biblical reference. I will use stories from history to show the ongoing nature of a truth. I do not use canned stories, though I think they are useful for some. I prefer to draw from the material I have experienced and to rely on the supportive truths that emerge.

I must return to the three elements that define for me the sermon: the setting, the character, the incident. Once I have finished my research, I then decide where I will focus the introduction. I will normally take the antithesis of the truth I am presenting and then work my way to the thesis. It is at this point that the drama begins and the screenplay takes over. The sermon can start in the historical moment or in the contemporary setting. That for me is not the issue. I want to introduce the drama. I try to make sure that the setting, the context for the story, is clear, and then I present the characters that will dominate the presentation. What I have gleaned about them—their problems, their idiosyncrasies, their struggles, and their hopes—are now painted with words on the canvas of the minds of the hearers. I want the hearers to feel as if they know the characters and to feel as if they can identify with them.

The incident brings this to a head, because the incident is a situation faced by a *certain kind of person,* the one presented in the sermon. Why is David more upset with Nabal than Saul? Why does Noah get drunk when he has so great a challenge? Why does Judas betray Paul? How does Job bear up under the strain? If the story is told correctly, the setting put in its context, the character laid bare and the incident held up to the light, then new understanding about God, life, and our struggle emerges. Christ is seen in the story, but he is also seen as one among *us.* The story becomes alive as the eternal truths that are hidden in the story break forth. It is as if we have gone to a movie and the writer has stayed after to tell and give all the clues and truths that are buried within the story. I guess this is part of my fascination with preaching. I just love the truths that are there.

It has been said that preachers are really philosophers talking about the principles of life. I really think we are more than that. We are not students of logic and semantics. We do not spend hours upon hours wrestling with ontological propositions. We wrestle with life. We struggle with meaning in life. We look for God in the places others have written off. We are discoverers on a mission, and when we make a discovery, we race back to show it off to everyone.

Before concluding, there is one more preaching element I must address. It is *humor.* Life to me is not a tragedy. Regardless of the goings on, the story never ends in tragedy. There may be ups and downs; there may be a need to see a bigger view; but the story is never going to end in despair. For me there is *always humor.* I use humor as comic relief and as a way of helping us laugh at ourselves. Humor helps to loosen up our minds and thoughts so that God can penetrate them with new ideas. I seldom preach a sermon that does not have humor. I have found that the drama of life is extremely diverse. Tears, laughter, frustration, shouts of acclamation, intelligence, stupidity, baseness, honor, and so much more invite us to come and spend time with them. All of these emotions have been in my story and are a part of the stories of those who hear the word. I have found that laughing and crying can be a part of the same sermon.

I try to make sure that I have my sermon text for the next week by the end of Sunday. When I am preaching a series, I will outline the entire series and work on each segment one week at a time. I will try to have my thoughts clear by no later than Tuesday so that Wednesday and Thursday can be spent exploring my references. I do not use commentaries unless there is a point at which I am stuck. On Thursday morning I start my writing, and I write until I finish. I do not do drafts. I write from start to finish, and then I am finished. Though I write some sermons on the computer, the majority are written out in longhand. There is something about the feel of the pen and seeing the words on the paper that still moves me. It is a great relief to end Thursday with my sermon finished. I seldom if ever write on Saturday nights. My friend James Perkins said if you don't have a sermon by then, "give God a rested body and a clear mind." On a couple of occasions I have had to do that.

My two sons are following me in this preaching ministry, and I pray to God they will glean from their father but will also add their own contribution to the study of preaching. It is so marvelous a craft, so unexplored, and so engaging that I cannot wait to see how others will approach it. In the end, there is but one story, *His Story*, and we are blessed to be in the fellowship of those entrusted to tell it.

Sermon: "Take a Journey with Me"
Matthew 4:18–22

WALTER S. THOMAS SR.

The master is not a rich man. He is not a part of the landed gentry. He is not a member of the aristocracy. He is a lowly carpenter from the ghetto community of Nazareth. He is a poor man with a powerful presence and an amazing anointing. He does not have much to offer in the way of worldly resources, yet he is able to muster heaven and make even the elements obey his will. I would have loved to have been there when he performed those miracles. He was a man so completely together that power had no problem bending to his will. It is still true that God will only allow his power to flow where God's purposes are honored.

The Gospel narratives each seek to share the beginnings of the Master's ministry, and it is clear that it began with miraculous demonstrations. Mark talks about healings; John talks about water being turned into wine; and Luke talks about the casting out of demons. Matthew, however, assumes that we are aware of the power of his early introduction and begins his story with the Master's invitation to people of potential to come and take a journey. He is not inviting them to be saved; he is inviting them to take a marvelous and exciting journey. You see, all some people want is the *transaction* of salvation. In the words of that gospel favorite "Amazing Grace," "I once was lost but now I am found." Yet there are others who want more than just to know they are saved and that their sins are forgiven. They want to know and to experience the life of Christ flowing through them. Matthew starts the Gospel by saying that Jesus is inviting us to take a ride with him and to see where it takes them.

How important that place of beginning really is. God is starting the journey with but one thing, an invitation: Come and journey with me. In order to journey with him we must overcome (1) *our dependence on what we know* because he will expose us to a dimension we have never known. He is the Lord God of Wonders. We must overcome (2) *our fear of ourselves* because he will help us to see a greatness we did not know we had. Finally we must overcome (3) *our desire to secure ourselves* because our security is in God and God alone.

TRANSITION

It is by the Sea of Galilee that the story begins. The Master has, according to Luke, already held class and taught lessons. Now he walks by the sea and makes an outright invitation to some men to change the direction of their lives. They are gainfully employed. They have families. They have careers and reputations; yet the Master does not hesitate to invite them to put all of that behind them and launch out on an uncertain path with an unknown guide. The question is not how could he ask them to leave their lives and make this move, but the real question is what prompted them to say, yes? Do not think that people have it together and are satisfied with their lives simply because they have a job, a house, a car, and so forth. Do not believe that everyone who works is happy or that everyone walking and breathing has found purpose and meaning. The truth is that there are many persons who would trade what they have for just one minute, one day, or one hour of meaning, understanding, and genuine purpose.

First, Jesus encounters Peter and Andrew as they are mending the nets. They are fishermen, but he offers them an opportunity to take a ride with him. He comes across James and John and also asks them to leave their lives and follow him, and they do so immediately. Their response cannot be glossed over. They immediately dropped what they were doing and followed him.

They are anxious for something different, and they knew it when it arrived. I want to say to some young adults and even to adults, be willing to admit that you need something more than what you have, and when the Lord offers, be sure to step up. They immediately left their boats and their families and followed him. The journey was about to start and in the words of our theme, "Our Journey Starts Now!"

It is high time we realize just what the Lord is offering and why we ought to answer in the affirmative. It is time we learned that the gift he sends our way is more precious than anything we have ever had or imagined. It is time to muster whatever we need to muster and to get on board the Master's train. I am lifting this today because so many of us stop with just salvation and miss the joy and the excitement that goes along with journeying with Jesus. With Christ, there is much to be experienced, to know, and to understand. We cannot let this moment pass. We do not come here week after week to hear sermons or to socialize. We do not come here for choir selections or marching ushers. We come because a journey has begun and we want to take it and enjoy it to the fullest. We are here to become everything that the Lord says is possible for us, and it can be accomplished in spite of every obstacle that is put in our path and every trial that comes our way. *We cannot afford to miss this opportunity.*

I.

Jesus says take this journey with me because you are about to see *the glories of the kingdom!* As we read the narratives of the Gospels it is clear that the disciples, those who walk with the Master, see the mighty work of God at each and every turn in life. They see God moving in ways that are unbelievable and unimaginable. They are permitted to witness the very moves of God when he makes them, and they see the effects of those moves. What do I mean? They see that

the blind see.

the lame walk.

the dead are called back to life.

the hungry are fed.

the weary are lifted.

the sorrowing are made glad.

They see miracle upon miracle, and they are witnesses to the Lord's battle with evil for the hearts and destiny of humankind. They see God use power to free captives and to make broken men whole. What happens is that *they see more than life wants them to see.* Life wants us to see only the pain and the suffering, but God wants us to see the wonders and the miracles that will inspire and motivate us:

Women are made whole.

Children are given hope.

Persons vested in the system break ranks and follow him.

Wounded souls are made whole.

Frightened persons find faith and stability.

They saw

the winds and the waves calmed.

the five thousand fed.

the lame walking.

Jairus's daughter walking.

Lazarus rise from the dead.

Legion made into a functioning man of dignity and with respect.

I must admit, I am excited to be a saved soul on a journey with Jesus. I, too, can say I have things too wonderful to describe. I have seen

demons fall.

liars confess.

ways made out of no way.

dollars multiply.

mountains leveled.

valleys exalted.

ninth-hour victories.

last-minute deliverances.

in-the nick-of-time liberations.

The history of our world and our times is that we see pain and misery everywhere we look. The media makes its money on despair and bad news. Simply put, "bad news sells." Yet to begin to see life through a different lens, a positive lens, a lens of opportunity, requires that we be *with him* for this to happen. When we are with him, the eyes of our understanding are opened. The Lord offered to his twelve the same thing that he is offering to us. He wants us to see the world as God created it for us. He wants us to see the things that are missed, the opportunities that are not taken, and the thrills that are around the corner. He showed it to the disciples and offers to show it to us. It requires a different mind-set. It requires an acceptance of the impossible as possible, and it requires a faith in God that longs for the unimaginable. I must admit, I understand the words of the gold gospel song "Every day with Jesus" much better now than I did years ago: "Everyday with Jesus is sweeter than the day before." He has continued to make me stand astonished at what he does and how he does it. These men would leave their nets and wind up with so much power that their shadows would bring healing. He is offering to those sharing this word the same experience: "Come see the wonders!"

II.

They traveled with him and as such they were blessed to *learn the truths of the kingdom*. They not only saw the glories of the kingdom; they were blessed to hear the Master teach and to have him teach them personally. Too many persons think that we are just learning Bible verses and memorizing Scriptures; they do not realize that we are learning the keys to access power and manifest the things of the kingdom. The words we learn from him we speak in the situations that come our way, and we find them to have the power that is needed for liberation. It is not just some rote memorization. We are blessed to have learned the things that are vital to continue his works. We learn that his words provide us with *access to power*. His truth creates opportunities for us and makes room for us. He provides opportunities that are beyond our imagination. His truth aligns forces and gives us the support we need in every situation. Angels come to our rescue. The Holy Spirit empowers our minds and hearts with insights and understandings. His truth directs resources for us to use in each and every encounter. He provides!

Look at the twelve disciples. They traveled with the Master, hearing him teach parables and heal the brokenhearted. They sat with him in private places and heard him expound on truth and expand their understanding. He was their teacher, and they rejoiced in being his students. I see them waiting and watching to see what would be the next manifestation that would lead them to revelation. They walked with him, and he shared the truths that gave his life substance and strength. They saw glories and learned truths, but after the Master left them the work and filled them with his spirit, those words were activated in them, and they were able to fully continue the work. The truths that the Master shares with us can lead us to "march into hell for a heavenly cause."[1] They are life and spirit. We live by that word, and we stand by that word. When we journey with Jesus and he teaches us the truth of the kingdom, we become filled with the *rhema* and the *logos* word that will empower everything we do. He gives us his truths so that we can have his life in us. His word is life and life more abundant.

There is no way to understand our progress as a people without seeing the mighty hand of God moving upon our lives. Liberation is the result of a word spoken that did not return void. In the darkness of the moment, we often did not see the light, but those who spoke in faith and hope knew the strength of the master's words and held us tight until the light shone upon our path. We are who we are because someone took the word seriously and stood upon its truth and acted. We learned that what he did he will also do through us.

Too many of the saints miss the very power of knowing the word and the strength that it releases. My God, even the Twenty-third Psalm can carry you through a difficult place and help you stand in the toughest of situations. Jesus asked his Father to sanctify us through truth, but he said, "Thy word is truth" (John 17:17). It is the word that gives us

clarity of vision.
the power of purpose.
the strength to struggle.
victory over defeat.
the love for living.
the hope for every tomorrow.
the courage to face evil.
determination to fight oppression.

Do not underestimate the power of the word in your life. It will

hold you.
convict you.
correct you.
challenge you.
comfort you.
call you.
constrain you.
strengthen you.
empower you.
enrich you.
encourage you.
instruct you.

Learn this word, and let it change your life. That is the promise of Jesus as we journey with him. If we take his word to heart and hide it in our hearts, we will understand what has been hidden from us. I can see into his eyes that look of love, hope, and excitement as he taught them to use the keys to the kingdom. He wanted them to know the Father as he knew him and to experience all that was possible. His voice dripped with anticipation when he said, "Follow me," and they sensed it and heard it and left their nets to be with him.

III.

He says travel with him and know *the hope of kingdom.* You see as they traveled with him they began to understand that God was offering something both *in the here and now* and *the not yet.* What these disciples were about to learn was that the world they were in and the lives they were living were just one aspect of the kingdom of God. Once they let their lives be connected to Jesus Christ, they were then a part of something so much larger. Something that even life, as we know it, could not contain. He was bringing them into the very hope of the kingdom. The hope of the kingdom is that the world as we know it with all of its corruptions will one day become all it should be. We do not say that and sit idly by waiting for it to happen on its own. To the contrary, we fight to make it happen, and we labor to bring it to pass. We stand to serve. Yet the battles do not deter us or diminish our vigor or our efforts. We know that there is more than defeat and despair. There is hope, and even if we are not alive to see it come to pass on this side, we are a part of it on the other side.

That is the message of Jesus from the cross. He said, "It is finished" (John 19:30). His part was finished and yet the battle would continue to rage. His part on the cross was over, but his next date was with a resurrection. *There is always something waiting for us when we journey with him.* I love how Paul spoke of it:

> To be absent from the body, and to be present with the Lord (2 Cor. 5:8 KJV)

> For we know that if our earthly house of [this] tabernacle were dissolved, we have a building of God, a house not made with hands, eternal in the heavens. (2 Cor. 5:1 KJV)

And Jesus said,

> Let not your heart be troubled; . . . 'in my Father's house are many mansions. . . . I go to prepare a place for you' (John 14:1 KJV)

The journey with Jesus makes us a part of something big and meaningful, the kingdom of God. We talk about the church and our organizations, but Jesus talked about the kingdom and came to usher it in. The kingdom has men and women of every race and from every nation. It has the high and the low, the rich and the poor, the learned and the unlearned. We are all a part of the great hope of the kingdom. We come together in his name. The disciples were now a part of this, and we too have been baptized into the kingdom. He wanted them to join him, first learning and then doing. Now we are in the same tradition. We are learning, but we will be doing. We will do the things of which he spoke. We will do the signs and wonders. We will speak the truth that reveals life and hope, and we will make manifest the kingdom of God. I know their hearts were overjoyed. They accepted. They said yes. They had no idea where it would lead, but they knew the end would not be on this side but in glory.

I do have an expectation and anticipation that one day I will see the fullness of all I have come to know exists. We do not talk about it, but we should. This is not the end. There is a place where the wicked shall cease from troubling. There is a place where the presence of God never fades. There is a place where the power of his love always shines. There is a place where wickedness is banished and trouble is no more. There is a place. I hear him say, Take this journey with me, and it *will* end in glory. I am going all the way. I do not plan to get off until my feet strike the shores of the new kingdom. I am going all the way with Jesus!

10

Devotion to Delivery

MELVIN V. WADE SR.

Before I ever had the chance to sit in classes dealing with homiletics, hermeneutics, or sermon preparation, I had the favored privilege of sitting at the feet of some of the greatest African American preachers of all times. Let me just name a few: my own late father and mentor, Dr. J. C. Wade Sr.; Dr. J. H. Jackson; Dr. Gardner C. Taylor; Dr. C. A. W. Clark; Dr. C. L. Franklin; Dr. Manuel L. Scott; Dr. J. P. Barber; Dr. F. Benjamin Mays, and Dr. Sandy F. Ray. As I listened to these preaching giants, I began to see and sift what was the secret of their preaching prowess. I found that there was an amalgamation and a syncretism of Bible, prayer, power, rare in-depth scriptural insight, theology, contextual imagination, oratory, illustrations, and celebration. Let me hasten to add that preachers who had no opportunity to hear these men are all the poorer.

Young preachers in those days were cautioned to academia. However, we were also challenged to make our goods marketable. We were told not to take our goods out of the freezer and put them on the table, but to take them by the fire. We were further informed not to major in gravy but to major in good cuts of meat, with the guaranteed assurance that a good cut of meat would make its own gravy.

I would hear Manuel Scott talk about the fact that he was a student of Harry Emerson Fosdick. I would hear Caesar Clark talk about D. Elton Trueblood. I came to find out that my father was reading Origen. I used to hear Gardner Taylor talk about Paul Scherer and

G. Campbell Morgan. And I used to hear my college dean talk about the fact that Paul Tillich was one of his instructors. From that, I started trying to read and digest these scholars that I had heard my preaching mentors talk about. Consequently, some of the insights that I gathered from reading these prolific writers, along with some others like Harvey Cox, Karl Barth, Leslie Weatherhead, Paul Tournier, and Reinhold Niebuhr, caused me to become topical in my presentation. I recall preaching messages such as "Humpty Dumpty," "Little Boy Blue," and "Ain't No Love in the City." With these and other titles like them, I thought I was really doing some great preaching until my brother, J. C. Wade Jr.—who, incidentally, God used to keep me alive when I received his bone marrow in a transplant after being diagnosed with leukemia—shockingly said to me, "Brother, if you don't know your Bible, you will never really lead God's people."

I had another challenging experience in a deacon's meeting in the early 1980s. I had a deacon literally whip me with the Bible while trying to get me to preach from it more faithfully. At that particular juncture in my ministry, I had to confront some things. First of all, I had to come to grips with the fact that I really didn't know the Bible. Second, I had to be honest and say that I read the Bible for the sole purpose of sermon preparation. Third, my messages were building a theological church and not a biblical church. It was during the 1980s that my late dear friend E. K. Baily encouraged me to learn the expositional method of preaching. Through his constant embrace, coupled with the exemplary preaching of A. Louis Patterson, my preaching began to bend its way to expository preaching. After reading books on sermon preparation and delivery by Jerry Vines, I began seeking books by other expositional authors. I began reading Warren Wiersbe, J. B. Philips, Ivor Powells, and James Montgomery Boice.

There was one last piece in my evolving preaching regimen. Even though I was doing expositional preaching, I found that I was still reading my Bible only for sermon preparation. However, in 1999 I was diagnosed with leukemia, and with death staring me in the face—having been informed that bone marrow transplants for African American males were not that successful—I began for the first time reading the Bible devotionally.

I've since come to this stark realization: that as witnessing follows worship, so biblical preaching follows biblical devotion. Before I begin making preparation for any sermon, the genesis point is daily, private devotion. I have shared my testimony in some conferences and seminars lately because devotional reading of the Bible seems to be a missing link. I would like to suggest that daily, private devotion is not some mere ineffective, optional extra. In fact, daily, private devotion should really be classified as an irrefragable, axiomatic sine qua non. The term *irrefragable* means "impossible to deny or refute." The word *axiomatic* means "a truth so obvious it needs no proof." And *sine qua non* means "an essential or absolute indispensible." Private devotion is thus an irrefutable, obvious essential for any preacher.

A very insightful psalm that I learned from memory early on is the First Psalm. It reads, "But his delight *is* in the law of the LORD; and in his law doth he meditate day and night" (Ps. 1:2 KJV). Richard Foster, in his book *Celebration of Discipline*, makes three specific statements that I find to be germane at this juncture. First, he says, "Today there is an abysmal ignorance of the most simple and practical aspects of nearly all the classic spiritual disciplines." Second he says, "To know the mechanics does not mean that we are practicing the discipline." And then third, he notes, "The inner attitude of the heart is far more crucial than the mechanics for coming into the reality of the spiritual life."

For me, it took divine, sovereign orchestration of devastation that came in the form of a bone marrow transplant to bring me to the realization of the vitalness, the richness, and the power that exudes from the simple discipline of daily devotion. I had to agree with the psalmist as he wrote in Psalm 119:71 (KJV), "*It is* good for me that I have been afflicted; that I might learn thy statutes." It was during this time that I really came to grips with the priority of daily devotion. The idea of what God in his sovereignty permitted, reminded me of a story that I had heard years ago:

A boy made himself a boat and went down to the lakeside to try it out. Because of the undercurrent and waves of the lake, the boat got beyond the reach of the little boy. All of a sudden, the boy noticed that his older brother was throwing rocks at the boat. The little brother went to fight his older brother to stop him from throwing at the boat. When the younger brother reached the older brother, the older brother, lovingly, wrapped the younger brother in his arms and turned him around. When the younger brother turned around, he beheld his boat coming back to the shore. The older brother began telling the younger brother, "You thought that I was throwing at your boat. I was not throwing at your boat trying to destroy your boat, but I was throwing beyond your boat trying to create

enough ripples and waves in the water to bring your boat back to
the shore."

I realized that that was exactly what happened to me. God sent me
through leukemia and a bone marrow transplant not to destroy me but
to bring me closer to him through the means of daily devotion—to
empower me and to prepare me to proclaim his gospel. I recognize that
I have spent considerable time in the area of daily devotion, but I must
say that I cannot express the valuable significance of daily devotion. In
2 Kings 5, Naaman almost missed healing from the deadly disease of
leprosy because he did not want to deal with simplicity. In Mark, chapter 9, the nine disciples found themselves impotent and powerless
because of their failure in the simple areas of fasting and praying.

I know that daily devotion would not be labeled or classified under
the headings of some of the weightier subject matters, but I suggest that
to pass over how weighty daily devotion is, is to pass over not only the
power to preach but even the *something* to preach. Just as worship has a
powerful effect on witnessing, so daily devotion has a similarly powerful
effect on sermon preparation and sermon delivery. To neglect the simple
discipline of daily devotion is to neglect the very essence of preaching,
which is power, preparation, and proclamation. Furthermore, the
inevitable and ultimate outcome of our daily devotion is knowing what
sermon or series of sermons to preach. I used to spend a considerable
amount of time hunting for something to preach. Now I don't have to
hunt for sermon ideas. Somehow God, in his own sovereign, mysterious
way, reveals what he wills for me to preach as the inevitable fruit of my
communing and having holy intimacy with him through the means of
daily devotion. Daily communing with God becomes the guarantee that
God will reveal what it is that he wills and wants his servant proclaimers
to preach. So, succinctly, my first step in sermon preparation is daily
devotion.

Once it is revealed to me *what* to preach, I then engage in the dual priority of reading the passage and praying for guidance and revelation. First
of all, I read the text continuously because I want to familiarize myself
with it. I then try to see if I need to read the previous passage or the suc-
ceeding passage in order to get the context and understanding of the
story. It is quite clear that narratives are easier to grasp than the theological treatise that Paul gives in books like Romans, Galatians, and Eph-
esians. The difficulty of the passage thus becomes the determining factor
as to how many times I read a text in order to become familiar with it.

After becoming familiar with the text, I reread it to see if I can easily summarize what the passage is about. For example, I preached a message from 1 Samuel 28. It's the story about Saul seeking the witch at Endor in order to speak to Samuel. In attempting to recapitulate the story, I began to see that the story was about God's firing Saul. God refused to talk with Saul, because through perpetual, defiant rebellion Saul had degenerated from God's anointed to God's enemy. And the tragedy of it all was that Saul didn't know that he had been fired. I seek to familiarize myself with the text so that I can retell the very gist of the story in a few sentences, as I have tried to do in the above illustration.

This idea of becoming familiar is an ultraessential concept. I have noticed that in the sports world, sports teams encourage teammates to spend more time with each other, not only during practice time, but before and after practice. In fact, teammates are encouraged to spend time with each other after the season has ended. Again, the underlying goal is for them to become familiar with one another.

Prior to my marriage, my wife, Jacquie, and I did not go from the introduction by my friend E. K. Bailey to planning our wedding. We spent considerable time becoming familiar with each other. We did that talking continuously on the phone, meeting for lunch at the student cafeteria, walking each other to class, going to church, going to the movies, sitting and chatting in the student center or out on the school yard, and attending athletic games and school functions together. Our romance and marriage did not just happen, nor was it fortuitous. Rather than being a quantum leap, it was slow and incremental.

In like fashion, the idea of being familiar with the text should never be undervalued. There should be holy familiarity and holy intimacy with the text. And that takes one's prime time. I recall reading in a magazine a cartoon where the pastor lived next door to the church. Finally, one day, the deacons and trustees went to the pastor and asked him when did he prepare his sermons. The pastor responded by saying that he prepared his sermons between the house and the church. At the next meeting of the deacons and trustees, they bought the pastor a house forty-five minutes from the church.

These church leaders were able to see that it takes some time to put a sermon together. In like fashion, it takes time to become familiar with any particular text. And over the years, in rereading or further familiarizing yourself with a text, inevitably you will see something that you had not seen in previous readings. Therefore, I would poignantly urge that the idea of becoming familiar with a passage not be downplayed. Familiarity with a passage is an ultraessential.

Synchronous or simultaneous with familiarity with the text ought to be strong prayer. The God who calls us and gifts us with assignments is the God of disclosure and revelation. The report is that there are 31,174 verses in the Bible. The report says that "the middle verses of the Bible are the 15,587th and the 15,588th verses of the Bible." That makes Ps. 118:8–9 the middle verses of the Bible. They read,

> "*It is* better to trust in the LORD than to put confidence in man.
> *It is* better to trust in the LORD than to put confidence in princes."
> (KJV)

I mention that because one of the great temptations of sermon preparation is to seek human commentaries rather than to seek disclosure, revelation, and guidance from God. Solomon writes in Prov. 3:5–6,

> Trust in the LORD with all thine heart; and lean not unto thine own understanding.
> In all thy ways acknowledge him and he shall direct thy paths.
> (KJV)

The God of revelation should never be bypassed in favor of commentaries. I'm not contending that there should be an either/or; I contend that it should be both/and. The Bible represents the mind and wisdom of God in print whereas the writers of the commentaries exegete the text. However, God deals on a higher plain because God does what only God is able to do—that is, God is able to exegete God. Thus, it would seem the best possible thing to do is consult first with the one who is able to give us the greatest exegesis—that would be God.

Another thing to keep in mind is an idea that we have been taught through the years: God has three significant or essential words. One is the living Word, which we know to be Jesus. The second word is the written Word, which we know to be the Bible. And the third word is the proclaimed Word, which we know to be the preached Word. The Living Word, Jesus, is God manifested in the flesh. The written Word is God's using holy men to write his mind and will as he gave utterance. What this means is that the sine qua non of our preaching is God. Therefore, God should never be our secondary source. God should always be the primary source that we consult first.

One time I looked at the term *preach*, and I began erasing the first letter just to see what it would look like. You start with *preach*, and if you continue erasing first letters, it narrows down to *reach*, then *each*, and then *ach* (phonetically, the "e" is silent in the word "ache.") God, the God of revelation and disclosure, is both omniscient and omnisapient. *Omniscient* is all-knowing, and *omnisapient* is all-wise. Knowing is information, and wisdom is right application. Commentary authors may be brilliant in their insights, but only God is omniscient and omnisapient.

When we couple the idea of *preaching* with the idea of "reaching each ache," we might conclude that commentary writers know the exegesis of the text, but only the omniscient, omnisapient God knows the aches and has the wisdom to reach the aches. Inasmuch as the omniscient God knows the aches and has the omnisapience to apply the right remedy to alleviate the ache, then through the means of perpetual prayer, God ought to be consulted first.

After reading and digesting the text so that I have developed a holy familiarity with it—and after much fervent, perpetual prayer—I begin to seek a subject that I believe will do several things. First, I seek a subject that will, in a composite, succinct, abridged fashion, capsulize the whole passage and keep the passage contextually true. I remember reading years ago about the idea of "having a well in a drop." To me, the subject ought to be a well in a drop that always keeps the passage contextually true.

For example, in Matthew 20, Jesus tells a parable about the workers who were hired to go into the vineyard and work at varied intervals beginning at 6:00 a.m. with the hiring at 5:00 p.m. The subject that I used was "Grumbling about Grace." To me, this subject capsulized the whole context of the parable, which connects back to a question that Peter raises in Matthew 19. Peter's inquiry was concerning what the disciples should have as a result of being on the ground floor of the Lord's kingdom and as a result of what they had given up to follow Jesus. Peter was ultra concerned, as I'm sure the others were also, about kingdom remuneration. Jesus retorts by telling the parable of Matthew 20, wanting his disciples, yea even us today, to understand that kingdom remuneration is not earned or merited but is solely based on grace. And if anybody dares to complain about what they have received, they are grumbling about grace.

Not only do I seek a subject that is a well in a drop and contextually true to the passage, but I look for a subject that is an attention grabber.

I have always been taught that you have only a few minutes to capture the attention of the people to whom you preach, and a part of the first few minutes is the subject of the sermon.

The subject should also tell the listeners what exactly they ought to be listening for. The Bible classifies our listeners as sheep, and one of the things that sheep need, because of their dimsightedness, is leading. In Psalm 23, for example, the sheep are constantly being led. Therefore, we have the awesome responsibility of leading the sheep in what to look for as we feed them. The subject is thus not just designed to capture their attention, but it ought to be telling them what to look for as they hear the Word of God.

During the time of my transition from topical and textual/topical preaching to expository preaching, before the biblical word study and computer programs were introduced, I was introduced to the writings of Kenneth Wuest. Though the books dealt with New Testament studies, it caused me to look for material that gave insights on key terms in the passage, not just the text at large. After being introduced to Wuest, I was introduced to *Vine's Dictionary of Biblical Words*. Again, this sent me looking for key terms in the text. I have come to find out that examining key terms in a text can help to make all of the difference in the world by giving me clearer insights and clearer meanings into passages.

Several years ago I preached a sermon titled "What God Did for God on Mt. Calvary." What led me to this subject was the fact that I did a word study on Romans 3:25. Based on the definitions of the key terms and phrases of the verse, which are *whom, set forth, righteousness, for, remission, sins that are past,* and *forbearance.* After seeing the literal meaning of these words, I read the verse using the literal definitions. The verse then read, "Jesus Christ, whom God hath made plain or public, to be a propitiation or a reason for not executing deserved punishment through faith in his blood, to prove his moral, holy, and just character, on account of his intentionally passing over of sins, formerly committed, through the self-restraint of God." What this really proves is that in the very realest sense, God the Father is responsible for putting Jesus, his sui generis Son, on the cross in order for God to declare his righteousness.

Just reading the text without some word-study insight would not have revealed this fact. To further prove my point, I cited the term *remission.* Normally, the word *remission* means "dismissal, release, and pardon of penalty." Through word study, I found out that the word *remission* occurs only this one time in Scripture, and it is not the usual term for the idea of "remission." The word *remission* here is actually translated "pretermission." It was a Roman law term and meant that someone had been "overlooked, passed over, or disregarded intentionally." The definition of the term *remission* helps us to see that in this passage God intentionally overlooked and disregarded sins. Therefore, because we know that God hates sin, what we get is that God could intentionally disregard or pass over sins because in eternity past God had already slain the Lamb, and in time, God would pay the price of his Son in order to vent his wrath and satisfy his justice.

I remember hearing Dr. Harry S. Wright say, "The design of the preaching of the gospel is not to mystify people, but to clarify people." Also, I was instructed concerning people's retention. From studying the expository works of Dr. Jerry Vines, Dr. J. B. Philips, Dr. Warren Wiersbe, and Dr. James Montgomery Boice, I saw the need and purpose of outlining a passage so that it would be easy for listeners to remember, and because it provided a summary of the whole point that I was trying to make. Furthermore, as I studied the masterful work of Jesus, it was clear that Jesus used the most simple in order to reveal the most sublime. In my outlines, I thus seek to use the simple so that listeners don't have difficulty understanding. I follow the saying "Why preach if the hearers can't remember what you said?"

Let me use for my example an outline of the sermon that I shall use at the conclusion of my essay. The sermon is titled "The Gospel According to the Ants." My first outline point is "The Busyness of Ants." Proverbs 6:8 tells us what ants are busy doing. The second point is "The Fellowship of Ants." When Prov. 6:6 is coupled with Prov. 30:25, it becomes clear that ants do not work singularly but as a fellowship. The third and final point is "The Preparation of Ants." Proverbs 6:8 says that the ant prepares her meat in the summer. The idea is that through blind instinct, ants prepare for the future while the season is favorable.

The outline summarizes the text while at the same time, due to its simplicity helps the listeners recapture the very heart of the message. I'm sure I'm not the only preacher to have a listener recapitulate a message that they have heard based on an outline that they remember.

Let me conclude by mentioning two things that I use in sermon preparation to hammer home the points that I seek to make. One is clear illustrations. The second is what I call "runs." I shall give examples of both illustrations and "runs" in the sermon that follows. The purpose of both is to do what Dr. Gardner Taylor says in one of his classic sermons: to give "wide vision from narrow windows."

Sermon: "The Gospel according to the Ants"
Proverbs 6:6–8

MELVIN V. WADE SR.

In the text before us today, we find God resorting to the unorthodox and unconventional. We have some good news being transmitted and taught by ants. The kingdom of ants is making an infallible announcement. Apparently, Solomon notices something about the behavioral patterns of these insects of a hymenopteran species that needed to be observed. He noticed that the habits of the ants were didactic. He noticed that the ants have a message directed to the spiritually lazy. He wants the spiritual sluggard to observe the discipline, the diligence, and the methodology of ants. He wants the man who is neglecting his own spirituality to take careful notice of the behavior of ants.

I. THE BUSYNESS OF ANTS

Ants are always busy. Verse 8 tells us what they are busy doing. Ants are busy providing and gathering. Ants are feeble creatures, but they are always busy. Ants make use of every passing hour and are strict economists of time. It seems that the ants have some innate characteristic that has taught them that the inevitable tide of time is against them. Therefore, ants seem to make every moment count. It appears that the ant colony is built upon the twin principles and dual priorities of discipline and work. As a result, with skill, enthusiasm, and vigor, ants are always busy. And spiritual people, like ants, are feeble creatures that ought also to be busy. Have you ever noticed that in the Bible the Godhead never selects lazy or idle people? The Godhead always selects people who are busy doing something, even if the something that they were busy doing was wrong.

Jacob was busy being a trickster.

Rahab was busy being a prostitute.

Matthew was busy being a thief.

Simon the zealot was busy being an insurrectionist.

Saul was busy being a persecutor.

But God took these wrong-doing busy people, and with his salvific, metamorphosizing, transitioning, and revivifying power, entered into a mystical relationship with them. He changed their nature, sanctified and consecrated them, and used them in his service. One of the fundamental weaknesses of the church is that we have too many Christians who are not busy. It is sad that the church is loaded down and excessively stuffed with the lackadaisical, the insouciant, the nonchalant, the lazy, and the idle. But when we read the Bible, we shall discover that the call of Christ is to be involved. He makes it clear what the function of the redeemed is to be. He made it clear that if we are his disciples, we are the salt of the earth, the light of the world, and a city on a hill. He said that he had given to us the keys of the kingdom. He compared his work to that of bread and water. He said that the kingdom was like leaven. Now, when we look at these figures, we shall discover that they all have at least one thing in common. They all have the power of penetration. And likewise, we have been given the power to penetrate. Jesus said, "But ye shall receive power, after that the Holy Ghost is come upon you; and ye shall be witnesses unto me both in Jerusalem, and in all Judea, and in Samaria, and unto the uttermost part of the earth" (Acts 1:8 KJV).

II. THE FELLOWSHIP OF ANTS

A. Louis Patterson points out that in the Bible there is the law of first mention, fuller mention, and final mention. In Verse 6 of chapter 6 it says "her." That's first mention, but when we look at chapter 30 verse 25, portraying the wisdom of the small but mighty ants, it says, "They prepare their meat in the summer." That's fuller and final mention, which says that ants, though they are leaderless, do not work in solitude but work as a fellowship. Like the kingdom of ants, "the church of Christ is a fellowship." In the fellowship, there should never be division. There should always be unparalleled harmony and interrelatedness. There should be unparalleled harmony in the church not only because we are a fellowship but because we are more than a fellowship. Not only are we a fellowship but a family and a body. Jesus, knowing that we are a fellowship, a family, and a body, prayed, "Father make them one." What we must keep in mind is that Satan works in opposition to our unity. He seeks to work in an anonymous fashion through our narcissistic spirits to divide us. However, let me place this truth before us. Cut flowers don't last long.

III. FINALLY, THE PREPARATION OF ANTS

Ants prepare for the future. Verse 8 says that the ant provides her meat in the summer. Ants know that there is a summer and there is a winter. They know that the winter of the year is fast approaching. Therefore, ants, through the means of blind instinct, look ahead and make preparation while the season is favorable. However, careful examination of our human behavior patterns will reveal that unlike the ant, even though the season is favorable, our main concern is for this present world and not the future. Our thrust is on the earthly and the mundane. Our chief emphasis is on the new and the now. We make a lot of preparation for today, but I've come to say that, like the ants, we ought to start making plans for the future while the season is favorable. Since time is against us we had better make preparation for some place better while the season is favorable. Moreover, we know not the day nor the hour when the Son of Man shall come.

The story is told of a young woman who was hired as a live-in maid on a very rich estate. She was to cook, clean, and be a nanny and help raise the boss's children. Eventually, the parents who hired her died. But by then, the children whom she raised were grown and married. They remained in the mansion, and they had children whom she also raised. The children of the parents who hired her died, but she raised another generation of children. By then, she was no longer a young lady but an old woman. The second set of children that she raised had a family meeting and decided to let this old woman, whom they called "Auntie," go. After telling her they had to let her go and find someone much younger, they asked her what she wanted them to do for her. She said, "Call me a cab." She went upstairs to her room and packed her few little things in a box.

After coming downstairs with lines of tears meeting underneath her chin, she kissed everybody goodbye and went and got in the cab. The cab driver, whom she knew, asked her where she wanted to go. She said, "Go to the third light and turn left. Then go to the second light and turn right. Then go to the first stop sign and turn left." When he made the left turn at the stop sign, he started going up a hill. When he got to the top of the hill, she said, "Pull over and stop." When he stopped, he looked out of his window to the right and saw a vacant lot. He said, "Auntie, why do you want me to stop by this vacant lot?" She said, "You are looking in the wrong direction, look to your left." When he looked to the left, he saw a beautiful house with beautiful grass, trees, and flowers. The cab driver asked, "Who lives here"? She said, "I do." The cab driver said, "I thought you lived back down there at the mansion." She said, "No, I just worked down there, but I knew the day was coming when I couldn't work anymore, so I started making preparations."

I am like that woman. I work down here. I am a resident-alien. My business and work is ministry. But one of these days, my ministry will be over, and it will be moving time. When it's moving time, I have somewhere to go.

My father said, "It is a land of no mores," a land where there are

no storm clouds to rise.

no devil to tempt.

no wickedness to trouble.

no problems to solve.

no sorrows to share.

no death to die.

no tears to shed.

no grief to feel.

no more sickness.

no more pains.

no more night.

no more curse.

It's a land where Psalm 34 will take on eternal bliss. For "I will bless the Lord at all times: his praise *shall* continually *be* in my mouth" (KJV).

Notes

Chapter 3: Listening for God

1. Cynthia Rigby, "Lift Up Your Eyes on High and See" (keynote address, National Pastors' Sabbath, Salt Lake City, UT, June 2007).

2. Benjamin S. Baker, *Shepherding the Sheep* (Nashville: Broadman Press, 1983), 63–64.

3. Henri J. M. Nouwen, *The Wounded Healer* (New York: Doubleday, 1979), 94.

4. Howard Thurman, *The Negro Spiritual Speaks of Life and Death* (New York: Harper & Brothers, 1947), 21.

5. Robert J. Voyle, *Appreciative Inquiry* (Hillsboro, OR: Clergy Leadership Institute, 2006), 26.

6. Peter D. Kramer, *Against Depression* (New York: Penguin Books, 2005), 187–88.

7. Voyle, *Appreciative Inquiry*, 26.

8. Quoted in Barbara Brown Taylor, *Leaving Church: A Memoir of Faith* (New York: HarperCollins, 2007), 122.

Chapter 4: Rightly Dividing the Word

1. Allistair Begg, *Great Preaching: Practical Advice from Powerful Preachers* (Loveland, CO: Group Publishing, 2003), 23.

2. Rueben P. Job and Norman Shawchuck, *A Guide to Prayer for Ministers and Other Servants* (Nashville: The Upper Room, 1983).

3. Hannah Whitall Smith, *The Christian's Secret of a Happy Life* (New York: Fleming H. Revel, 1916), 40.

4. R. E. O. White, *A Guide to Preaching* (Grand Rapids: Wm. B. Eerdmans Publishing Co., 1973), 45.

Chapter 6: How I Prepare to Preach

1. Charles G. Adams, "Preaching from the Heart and Mind," in *Power in the Pulpit*, ed. Cleophas J. LaRue (Louisville, KY: Westminster John Knox Press, 2002), pp. 13–17.

2. Gardner C. Taylor, *Words of Gardner Taylor*, vol. 4, compiled by Edward Taylor (Valley Forge, PA: Judson Press, 2001), 140.

3. Rudolf Otto, *The Idea of the Holy* (London: Oxford University Press, 1923, 1950, 1957).

4. Paul Tillich, *Systematic Theology*, vol. 1, (Chicago: University of Chicago Press, 1951, 1956), 12–14.

5. Martin Luther King Jr., *Stride Toward Freedom: The Montgomery Story* (New York: Harper & Brothers), 134–35.

6. Harry E. Fosdick, *Riverside Sermons* (New York: Harper & Brothers, 1958), xi.

7. Martin Luther King Jr. *Letter from the Birmingham Jail* (San Francisco: Harper San Francisco, 1963, 1994).

8. Abraham Joshua Heschel, *The Prophets*. (New York: Harper & Row, 1962), 14.

9. Personal conversation with Rev. Jesse Jackson Sr., founder and president, Rainbow/PUSH National Coalition.

10. Personal conversation with the Reverend Dr. Joan Brown Campbell, director of religious life, Chatauqua Institution.

11. Desmond Bishop Tutu, *No Future Without Forgiveness* (New York: Doubleday, 1957).

12. Joseph Cardinal Bernardin, *The Gift of Peace* (Chicago: Loyola Press, 1997).

13. Harding, Vincent, Martin Luther King: *The Inconvenient Hero* (Maryknoll, NY: Orbis Books, 1996), 22.

Chapter 8: Preaching from the Overflow

1. Elwell, Walter A., and Barry J. Beitzel, *Baker Encyclopedia of the Bible* (Grand Rapids: Baker Book House, 1988), 631.

2. Ibid.

Chapter 9: The Power of Narrative Preaching

1. Don Quixote, "To Dream the Impossible Dream," *Man of La Mancha*.